"A WONDERFUL THING IS GOING TO HAPPEN"

A LITTLE MAID

OF

MASSACHUSETTS COLONY

BY

ALICE TURNER CURTIS

AUTHOR OF

A LITTLE MAID OF OLD PHILADELPHIA
A LITTLE MAID OF OLD NEW YORK
A LITTLE MAID OF MARYLAND
A LITTLE MAID OF OLD CONNECTICUT

ILLUSTRATED BY WUANITA SMITH

APPLEWOOD BOOKS
BEDFORD, MASSACHUSETTS

A Little Maid of Massachusetts Colony was first published by the Penn Publishing Company in 1914.

ISBN 1-55709-329-6

Thank you for purchasing an Applewood Book.
Applewood reprints America's lively classics—
books from the past that are still of interest to modern readers.
For a free copy of our current catalog, write to:
Applewood Books, Box 365, Bedford, Massachusetts 01730.

10 9 8 7 6 5 4

Printed and bound in Canada.

Library of Congress Cataloging-in-Publication Data
Curtis, Alice Turner.
    A little maid of Massachusetts Colony / by Alice Turner
Curtis; illustrated by Wuanita Smith.
        p.   cm.
    Summary: During the Revolutionary War, Anne Nelson jour-
neys with Indians, is imprisoned, escapes, and helps capture an
English privateer.
    ISBN 1-55709-329-6
    1. United States—History—Revolution, 1775–1783—
Juvenile fiction.   [1. United States—History—Revolution,
1775–1783—Fiction.   2. Massachusetts (Colony)—Fiction.]
I. Smith, Wuanita, ill.   II. Title
PZ7.C941Lme   1996
[Fic]–dc20   96-28380
                                              CIP
                                              AC

Introduction

THE first Anne Nelson story was *A Little Maid of Provincetown*, which told how the little Cape Cod girl's father went away to fight for the colonies, how she went to live with the Stoddards, how she escaped perils from Indians and wolves, made an unexpected trip to Boston, and carried an important message for the colonial army.

The girls and boys who made acquaintance in that book with Anne and with Amanda and Amos Cary will be glad to read here how Amos won his heart's desire,— to go a long voyage from the harbor of Province Town; Anne's journey with the Indians, her imprisonment in the house in the woods, and her escape; how she and Rose Freeman discovered "Aunt Anne-Rose" on the happy trip in Boston, and how Anne helped to capture an English privateer, will hold the attention of young readers, and, incidentally, show them something of the times and history of Revolutionary days in New England.

3

Contents

Illustrations

A Little Maid
of Massachusetts Colony

CHAPTER I

AMANDA'S MISTAKE

"Do you think I might go, Aunt Martha?" There was a pleading note in the little girl's voice as she stood close by Mrs. Stoddard's chair and watched her folding the thin blue paper on which Rose Freeman's letter was written.

"It is a pleasant invitation, surely," replied Mrs. Stoddard, "but the Freemans have ever been good friends to us; and so Rose is to visit their kin in Brewster and then journey back to Boston with her father in his chaise, and she says there will be plenty of room for you. Well! Well! 'Tis a wonderful journey."

Anne moved uneasily. "But, Aunt Martha, do you forget that she asks if Uncle Enos cannot bring me to Brewster?"

"Yes, child, I have read the letter, and I doubt not Enos will set you safe across to Brewster. And your father's vessel will be due in Boston early in September, and he could bring you safely home to Province Town. We'll see what Uncle Enos says about sailing across to Brewster," and Mrs. Stoddard smiled affectionately at Anne's delighted exclamation. It was two years before that Anne Nelson, whose father's boat had been seized by an English ship, had come to live with the Stoddards. Her father had escaped, and, after serving the colonies until after the battle of Lexington, had returned to Province Town, and was now away on a fishing cruise. Anne had visited the Freemans the year before, and now this pleasant invitation for a journey to Boston had been brought by one of the harbor fishermen, the only way letters came to Province Town. It was no wonder Anne was eager for permission to go. It would be a three days' ride from Brewster, and the road would take her through many pleasant towns and villages. There was not a person in the settlement who had taken the journey by land. Uncle Enos declared that Province Town folk who could sail a good boat, with fair winds, to Boston in six hours were too wise to take such a roundabout route as the land offered.

"But it will be a fine ride for Anne," he agreed. "She will learn much by the journey, and Squire Freeman will take good care of her. I'll set her across to Brewster on Tuesday, as Rose says they plan to start early on Wednesday morning. Well, Anne," and he turned toward the happy child, "what do you think the Cary children will say when you tell them that you are to ride to Boston in a fine chaise?"

"I do not know, but I think Amos will say that he would not journey by land; he is all for big ships; but I'm sure Amanda will think it is a wonderful thing, and wish to go with me, and indeed I wish she might. But why do we not have chaises in Province Town?"

"We must have roads first," replied Aunt Martha smilingly; "but Province Town has no need of coaches and roads with good boats in harbor. Now we must see that your clothes are in order, for a week soon goes."

"Anne! Anne!" and before Anne could respond a girl of about her own age came running into the kitchen. "Can you go with me over to the outer beach? May she go, Mrs. Stoddard? See! I have enough luncheon for us both in this basket," and Amanda held up a pretty basket woven of sweet grass.

"May I, Aunt Martha? And oh, Amanda! A wonderful thing is going to happen to me. Isn't it wonderful, Uncle Enos?"

Aunt Martha and Uncle Enos both smiled and nodded, and Amanda looked from one to the other in great surprise.

"Run along with Amanda and tell her all about it," said Mrs. Stoddard, and the two little girls started happily off.

"I can guess," declared Amanda, "for I know that Captain Starkweather brought you a letter from Boston, and I can guess who the letter is from."

Anne shook her head laughingly. "You would guess that it was from my dear father," she answered.

"And is it not?" questioned Amanda in surprise.

"It is from Rose Freeman," announced Anne. "And oh, Amanda, she asks me to come to Brewster next week, and go with her in her father's chaise to Boston!" And Anne turned, smiling happily, toward Amanda. She had expected Amanda to exclaim with delight over such a wonderful piece of news, but instead of delight Amanda's face expressed an angry surprise. She had stopped short, and stood looking at Anne.

"Rose Freeman!" she exclaimed. "Boston in a chaise! I wonder I play with you at all, Anne Nelson. Why don't you stay in Boston? I shouldn't care if you did!" and throwing the basket of luncheon on the ground Amanda turned and ran back toward home.

Anne looked after her in amazement. "That's the way she used to act before we were friends," she said aloud; "and all that good food thrown down in the sand," for the basket was overturned, and two round ginger cakes, two pieces of corn bread, and two three-cornered tarts had rolled out. Anne knelt down and picked them up carefully, shaking off the sand, and returned them to the basket.

"Her mother cannot afford to have such good things wasted," said Anne; for even the children in Province Town in the days of the Revolution knew how difficult it was to secure supplies. The end of Cape Cod, with its sandy dunes, scant pasturage or tillage, made the people depend on their boats, not only to bring in fish, but all other household necessities. The harbor was unguarded, and its occupation as a rendezvous by English men-of-war had made it very hard for the people to get provisions. So it was no wonder that Anne looked at the ginger cakes and tarts as special delicacies, too precious to lie in the sand.

"I'll go to the outer beach by myself," decided Anne, "but I will not eat my share of the luncheon. I do not see why Amanda should be angry," and the little girl walked on, choosing her way carefully among the scrubby pine trees or patches of beach-plum bushes.

Amanda ran swiftly, and in a moment or two was almost back in the Stoddards' dooryard!

"I mustn't go home," she said to herself; "they would question me, and I would have to tell them all the wonderful news about Anne. And, oh," she exclaimed aloud, "if I did not throw down the fine treat my mother put in the basket. I'll go back for it; Anne Nelson has everything, but she shall not have my tarts."

Amanda made her way back very carefully, hoping to get the basket and escape without Anne seeing her. But when she reached the spot where Anne had told the wonderful news neither the basket nor Anne was to be seen.

"She's run off with my basket. She means to eat all that mother gave me!" Amanda now felt that she had a just grievance against her playmate. "I'll go home and tell my mother," she decided, and on the way home a very wicked plan came into the little girl's mind. She pulled off her gingham sunbonnet and threw it behind a bunch of plum bushes. She then unbraided her neat hair and pulled it all about her face. For a moment she thought of tearing a rent in her stout skirt, but did not. Then she crawled under a wide-branched pine and lay down. "I must wait a time, or my mother will think I am too quickly back," she decided, "and I do not want to get home while Amos is there;" for Amanda knew well that her brother would not credit the story which Amanda had resolved to tell: that Anne had pushed her over in the sand, slapped her, and run off with the basket of luncheon.

"My mother will go straight to Mistress Stoddard, and there'll be no journeyings to Brewster to see Rose Freeman, or riding to Boston in a fine chaise," decided the envious child.

So, while Anne kept on her way to the outer beach, carrying Amanda's basket very carefully, and expecting every moment that Amanda would come running after her, and that they would make friends, and enjoy the goodies together, Amanda was thinking of all the pleasant things that a journey to Boston would mean, and resolving to herself that if she could not go neither should Anne. So envious was the unhappy child that she tried to remember some unkindness that Anne had shown her, that she might justify her own wrong-doing. But in spite of herself the thought of Anne recalled only pleasant things. "I don't care," she resolved; "she shan't go to Boston with Rose Freeman, and she has run off with the basket."

"Mercy, child! What has befallen you, and where is Anne?" questioned Mrs. Cary, as Amanda came slowly up to the kitchen door, where her mother sat knitting.

"She's run off with my basket," whimpered Amanda, holding her apron over her face.

"And is Anne Nelson to blame for your coming home in this condition?" questioned Mrs. Cary, a little flush coming into her thin cheeks.

Amanda nodded; some way it seemed very hard to say that Anne had pushed her down and slapped her.

"And run off with my basket," she repeated, "and next week she goes to Brewster, and by carriage to Boston."

"Well, that's no reason why she should turn so upon you," declared Mrs. Cary. "What made trouble between you?"

"I think it was because of this journey," replied Amanda. "She is so set up by it, and she went off with the basket."

"Never mind about the basket, child; but it's a sad thing for Anne to so lose her temper. You did quite right to come home, dear child; now brush your hair neatly, and bathe your face, and then come with me to Mistress

Stoddard; though I like not our errand," concluded Mrs. Cary, rolling up the stocking she was knitting.

Amanda looked at her mother pleadingly. "Why must I go to Mistress Stoddard's?" she questioned. "I have run all the way home, and you know she will not blame Anne; it will be me she will question and blame. Oh, dear!" and Amanda, sure that her evil plan would be discovered, began to sob bitterly.

"There, there! I did but think you could tell Mrs. Stoddard of Anne's mischief. You need not go, child. Get you a ginger cake from the stone jar in the cellar-way. I'll tell of the way Anne pushed you about, and made off with the basket, and you sit here by the door. There's a sweet breeze coming over the marshes," and, patting Amanda's ruffled locks, Mrs. Cary took down her sunbonnet from its hook behind the door, and prepared to set forth.

"I'll not be long away," she called back, as she passed down the sandy path.

From the pleasant doorway Amanda watched her with a gloomy face. Her plan was going on successfully, but Amanda did not feel happy. She was dreading the time when Amos would return, and his sharp questioning, she knew, would be a very different matter from her mother's acceptance of her story.

"Everybody always thinks that Anne is right," she said aloud.

"Well, isn't she?" said a voice directly behind her, so near that Amanda jumped up in surprise.

"How did you get into the house, Amos Cary!" she exclaimed angrily.

"Phew, Carrot-top! What's the matter?" responded Amos teasingly. "Say, Sis, don't cry," he added. "I won't call you 'Carrot-top' again. You know my hair's exactly the same color as yours, anyway; so it's just like calling myself names."

But Amanda kept on sobbing. "It's Anne," she whimpered. "She—she—she's run off with my basket."

"Anne!" exclaimed the boy in surprise. "Oh, well, she was only fooling. She'll bring it back. You know Anne wouldn't do a mean thing."

"She would, too. She's going to Boston, and to Brewster, with Rose Freeman," said Amanda.

"O-oh! So that's the trouble, is it?" said Amos. "Well, she'll come back, so don't cry," and he stepped past her and ran down toward the beach.

At Mrs. Stoddard's Mrs. Cary was repeating Amanda's story.

"I cannot understand it," said Mrs. Stoddard. "You know well, Mistress Cary, that Anne is a pleasant child, and she and Amanda started out as friendly as need be. Did Amanda say what began the trouble?"

Mrs. Cary shook her head. "No, she is at home crying her heart out about it, poor child."

"I know not what to say," and Mrs. Stoddard's usually smiling face was very grave. "Anne is not home yet, but I will question her. You may be sure, Mistress Cary, that I will not let it pass. Her father leaves her in my care when he is away, and perhaps I am too indulgent, for I love the child."

It was an hour later when Anne came and peered in at the open door. Mrs. Cary had gone home. Mrs. Stoddard looked at the little girl, but not with her usual smile.

"Where is Amanda's basket?" she asked sharply. "Do not stand there; come in." Anne obeyed. "Now, tell me why you pushed Amanda down, and slapped her, and ran off with the basket of food? Mrs. Cary has been here and told me all about it. A nice story indeed for me to hear. But like as not it is my fault for indulging you in everything. But I shall be firm now. Go up-stairs and stay until I call you; and as for that visit with Rose Freeman, think no more of it. I shall not let you go. No, indeed, after such a performance as this."

Anne thought to herself that she must be dreaming. "I shall wake up in a minute," she said aloud, but Mrs. Stoddard did not hear her.

"Go right up-stairs," she repeated, and Anne, with a puzzled look over her shoulder, went slowly up the narrow stairs.

CHAPTER II

ANNE DECIDES

"I DON'T know what to do," Anne whispered to herself, with a little sob, as she looked out of the narrow window in her little room. Captain Stoddard was coming briskly up the path; in a moment he would be directly under the window. "I'll call to him, and if he answers I shall know that I am awake," she decided, and leaning out she called softly: "Uncle Enos! Uncle Enos!"

Captain Stoddard looked up, and answered briskly: "Anne Nelson, ahoy!"

"Uncle Enos, listen!" and Anne leaned out still farther. "I went toward the outer beach with Amanda Cary, and she slapped me and ran off. And when I came home Aunt Martha sent me up-stairs. Now what have I done?"

Captain Stoddard chuckled, then he looked very serious indeed, and replied:

"A pretty affair! What have you been doing?"

"Nothing, Uncle Enos; indeed I have done no mischief. Tell Aunt Martha that Amanda slapped me, and that I did not slap back."

Uncle Enos nodded, and made a motion for Anne to be silent, and Anne drew quickly back into the room.

"Uncle Enos will find out," she whispered to the little wooden doll, "Martha Stoddard," that her father had made for her when she was a very small girl, and which was still one of her greatest treasures. But the July afternoon faded into the long twilight and no one called to Anne to come down. She began to feel hungry. "I wish I had eaten my share of that luncheon and not given it to Amos to carry home," she thought. For on her way home she had met Amos and had given the lunch basket into his charge, telling him to carry it home to Amanda, but saying nothing of Amanda's anger.

As Anne sat in the loft chamber waiting for the call that did not come, she began to feel that she had been treated very badly. "And Aunt Martha says I shall not visit Rose Freeman, and does not tell me why I shall not go. My father would let me; I know that full well. And I am going; I will walk to Brewster!" Anne's heart grew lighter as she thought of all the joys that a visit to Rose would mean. "I'll start tonight," she decided. "Maybe it will take me a long time, as there are no roads, but I know I can find the way. Oh, I wish it would get dark! I'll take you, Martha Stoddard, but I guess I'll change your name, for Aunt Martha doesn't like me any more," and the little girl began to feel very lonely and unhappy. The room door swung open at that very moment and there stood Mrs. Stoddard with a mug full of creamy milk and a plate of corn bread.

"Here is your supper, Anne. And I hope you are ready to tell me why you pushed Amanda down and ran off with her basket," and Mrs. Stoddard looked at Anne with a puzzled expression in her kind eyes.

"I did not —" began Anne.

"There, there, child. Mrs. Cary told me the whole story. Tell me the truth, and I'll not be hard with you," and Mrs. Stoddard set down the mug and plate on the light-stand and stood waiting.

"I will not say another word!" declared Anne, who felt that even her dear Aunt Martha had turned against her.

"Then you must stay up here until you are a more obedient child," said Mrs. Stoddard, and went slowly out of the room. "I don't see what has possessed the child," she said to Captain Enos on returning to the kitchen.

"She has always been a truthful child, Martha," ventured the captain, "so why not believe her now?"

"I would gladly, Enos; but Mrs. Cary came straight to me as soon as Amanda reached home, and 'twas an hour later when Anne returned, and she has no word of excuse. 'Twill do the child no harm to stay in her room until she can tell me the reason for such behavior. And of course this visit to the Freemans' must be given up. 'Twould not do to let her go after such conduct."

"A pity," responded the captain. " 'Twould have been a fine journey for the little maid."

Anne could hear the murmur of their voices as she drank the milk and ate the corn bread. "I wish I had some bread to take with me," she thought. "I'll take my blue cape, and my shoes and white stockings, for I'm sure I ought to wear them on the chaise," and

Anne tiptoed about the room gathering up her clothing. It did not make a very large bundle, even when she decided to take the white muslin dress, and the coral beads. She heard Captain Enos and Aunt Martha go to their chamber, and then, holding "Martha Stoddard" and the bundle in her arms, crept down the narrow stairway. The outer door stood ajar to admit the cool fragrant air, and in a moment Anne was running along the sandy track that led through the little settlement. It was still early, but there was not a light to be seen in any of the small gray houses. The summer sky was filled with stars, and as Anne ran she could see her shadow stretching ahead of her, "as if I were running right over it all the time," she whispered to "Martha Stoddard."

The beautiful harbor seemed like a shining mirror, it lay so calm and still in the shadow of the land. But Anne did not stop to look at stars or sea; she wanted to reach the pines at the end of the village. Then she meant to go on as fast as she could toward Truro. "There will be nice places to rest under the trees, where nobody will ever look for me; perhaps no one will want to look," thought the little girl, with a choky sensation in her throat as she remembered the strange happenings of the afternoon.

The track grew more indistinct toward the end of the settlement, and when Anne reached the woods the shadows were dark, and she was obliged to go carefully in order not to lose her way. The border line between Truro and Province Town was marked by the jawbone of a whale set in the ground by the side of a red oak stump. The path up to this landmark was well known to all the village children; the hill was called Cormorant Hill; and Anne had been there many times with Amanda and Amos and the Starkweather children, and was very sure that from that place she could find her way through Truro to Wellfleet. "I'll not rest until I get to Kexconeoquet," decided Anne. Kexconeoquet was the Indian name for the hill.

About half-way up the slope Anne stopped to rest under a tall pine tree. There was a bed of soft green moss, and as she sat down she gave a little tired sigh. "Maybe it will be morning before I get to the top of the hill," she thought, and put "Martha Stoddard" carefully down on the moss. "I suppose I might sleep a minute," she said drowsily, arranging her bundle for a pillow and resting her head upon it. And a moment later an inquisitive little squirrel noticed that there was a little girl in a brown gingham dress fast asleep under the pine tree.

Mrs. Stoddard awoke early the next morning, and when she and Captain Enos sat down to their simple breakfast she said:

"I hear no sound of Anne, and I'll let her sleep late this morning; when she wakes she will tell me what happened. I woke up in the night and thought about it, and

I feel sure our little maid could not have been all to blame. Amanda is quick to find trouble."

Uncle Enos nodded approvingly. " 'Twill do her no harm to sleep," he agreed, "and do not make up your mind that she must not go for the visit to Brewster and Boston. I can set her across to Brewster come Tuesday. 'Twill give me a chance to get some canvas for a new jib for the sloop."

Captain Enos spoke softly, and tiptoed out of the little kitchen, and Aunt Martha moved quietly about the house until the long summer morning was half over; then she went softly up the stairs, and opened the door to Anne's room. In a moment she realized what had happened: that Anne had run away; and she lost no time in hurrying to the shore, where Captain Enos was salting his yesterday's catch of fish and spreading them on the "flakes"—long low frames—to dry. Captain Starkweather and Amanda's father were near by, busy at the same work, and further along the shore were other groups of men taking care of the "catch" of the previous day. For the dried fish were shipped to many distant places, and curing them was a part of the fisherman's business.

"Anne is gone! She has run away," called Mrs. Stoddard, and in a moment she was telling Captain Enos that she was sure that the little girl had crept out of the house in the night. Captain Starkweather and Mr. Cary listened in amazement.

"But where could she go?" asked Captain Enos. "There's something wrong in this. Anne called to me from her window yesterday that she knew not the reason for her being punished. She has run away from us, Martha, because we have been unfair toward her."

"But where? Stop not to talk, Enos. Is there a boat missing? Like as not Anne has set forth for Boston." And Mrs. Stoddard looked out over the wide harbor as if expecting to see Anne sailing away.

"It may be your little girl is playing about and will soon return," suggested Captain Starkweather.

"Is her doll gone?" questioned Captain Enos; "for if it is not you may be sure that Anne is not far away."

"Indeed, I did not think to look; and you may be right, Captain Starkweather. I'll step back and see," and Mrs. Stoddard's face brightened as she turned toward home, followed by Captain Enos and the two fishermen.

"The doll is gone," she called down from the little chamber, "and Anne's cape and beads, and her shoes and stockings."

In a short time every one in the village knew of Anne's disappearance, and Amanda heard her father say that he feared Anne had started off in one of the little boats. "If she has there is small chance for the child," he said soberly, and Amanda began to whimper.

"She gave me Amanda's basket to bring home yesterday," said Amos; " 'tis in the shed."

"Yes, she ran off with it yesterday, and ate all the lunch herself," explained Mrs. Cary, "and slapped Amanda. Your sister came running home crying as if her heart would break."

"Anne didn't eat the luncheon. 'Twas all in the basket, and I ate it," said Amos. "I don't believe she slapped Amanda, anyway. Or if she did I'll bet Amanda slapped her first."

"Amos!" Mr. Cary's voice was very stern, and the boy said no more.

It was found that a rowboat was missing, and remembering how Anne and the Cary children had once started out to sail to Boston, it was generally believed that Anne had started off in the boat. Nevertheless search-parties went across the narrow strip of land to the outer beach and up and down the shore of the harbor and along the edge of the Truro woods. Several boats started off, for it was felt that the best chance of finding her was the hope that the little boat could not have gone very far. "It may have been swept out to sea," Mr. Cary said, and at this Amanda set up such a wail that he instantly added: "But Anne will be found; of course she will."

CHAPTER III

A NEW FRIEND

"It's morning!" And Anne sat up and looked about with surprised eyes. Little flecks of sunshine came through the sheltering branches of the tall pine, squirrels ran up and down its trunk, and there were chirpings and calls of birds among the near-by trees. "And I'm not half-way to the top," continued Anne, shaking off the feeling of drowsiness, and springing up from the soft moss. She picked up her bundle and "Martha Stoddard" and started on. " 'Tis about the time that Aunt Martha and Uncle Enos are eating porridge," she thought longingly, and then remembered that on the hillside, not far from the top, there was a spring of cool water, and she hurried on. She could hear the little tinkling sound of the water before she came in sight of the tiny stream which ran down the slope from the bubbling spring; and laying down her doll and the bundle she ran forward, eager for a drink. She knelt down and drank, and then turned to pick up her belongings, but the bundle and doll had disappeared. Anne looked about as if she could not believe her eyes. "They must be here!" she exclaimed aloud, and at that moment "Martha Stoddard" peered at her astonished owner from behind a tree. The little wooden doll appeared to walk. Then it bowed very low, and vanished. Anne ran to the tree, but Martha was not there; but the doll's head could be seen behind a small bush, almost within Anne's reach; but now Anne stopped, remembering that dolls, even dolls like Martha, could not play hide-and-seek. She felt bewildered, and, although Martha bowed and even tried to dance, Anne did not approach a step nearer. She could see that a small brown hand was keeping a tight grasp on Martha, and as she watched this hand a brown face peered out at her over Martha's head— the brown smiling face of an Indian girl, probably several years older than Anne. After looking at Anne for a few seconds she came out from behind the cluster of bushes. "She's as tall as Rose Freeman," was Anne's first thought.

"Where is my bundle?" she demanded, for although the Indian girl held Martha Stoddard in plain sight the bundle was not visible.

The Indian girl shook her head smilingly, and Anne repeated, "Bundle! Bundle!" and then exclaimed, "Oh, dear, she doesn't know what I say."

The girl now came a step or two nearer, holding out the doll for Anne to take. Her hair was very black and thick, and braided in one heavy plait. There was a band of bright feathers about her head, and she wore a loose tunic of finely dressed deerskin which came to her knees, and was without sleeves. Her arms and feet were bare, and as she stood smiling at Anne she made a very pretty picture.

Anne reached out her hand for the doll, and as she did so the Indian girl grasped it firmly, but in so gentle a manner that Anne did not draw back. The girl drew her along, smiling and saying strange sounding words in her own language, of which Anne could understand but one—"Mashpee." This was the name of a tribe of Cape Cod Indians who owned land, and who were always kind and friendly toward the white settlers; Anne was quite sure that the girl was telling her that she belonged to that nation.

The Indian girl circled around the big tree near the spring, and there lay—spread out on the moss—Anne's pretty blue cape, her white muslin dress, and her shoes and stockings and the bright coral beads. The Indian girl knelt down and picking up the beads fastened them about her own neck; she then threw the cape over her own shoulders, and, picking up the shoes and stockings, placed them in front of Anne, and put the muslin dress beside them.

It needed no words to explain this; she had selected what she wanted from the bundle and Anne could have the things that the Indian girl did not want.

Anne's face must have expressed what she felt, for the smile faded from her companion's lips, and the dark eyes grew unfriendly. She snatched the doll from Anne, and turned as if to run away.

"Nakanit!"

Both the girls gave a little jump, for they had been too much engrossed in each other to notice that an Indian squaw had come along the path, and had stopped a short distance from them. As she spoke the Indian girl started toward her, and began to talk rapidly. Anne stood waiting, and wondering what would happen now, and heartily wished herself safely back in the Stoddards' snug little house.

As the Indian woman listened Anne could see that she was angry and when Nakanit, for that was the Indian girl's name, had finished the squaw snatched the cape from the girl's shoulders, and, pointing to the beads, evidently bade her unfasten them. As the Indian girl obeyed the squaw gave her a sharp slap on the cheek, and Nakanit, without a look toward Anne, fled into the forest.

"Here, white child," said the woman, "here are your things. What are you doing so far from the settlement?"

"I am going to Brewster," replied Anne.

The Indian woman eyed her sharply.

"You have run away from your mother and father," she said sharply.

"My mother is dead, and my father is at sea," Anne replied, feeling her face growing red under the sharp eyes of the squaw, and a little ashamed that she did not own that she was running away from Aunt Martha

Stoddard. But she felt that Aunt Martha had been very unfair toward her.

The Indian woman's face softened. "And you journey alone to find friends in Brewster?" she asked.

"Yes, indeed; I am to go to Rose Freeman, and ride with her and her father in their chaise to Boston, and wait at their house for my father."

The squaw nodded. The name of Freeman was known to her, and though a sixty mile journey seemed a long way for so small a girl as Anne, the woman only wondered at the unkindness of the white women in letting a child go alone.

"Come," she said, and Anne, gathering up her shoes and stockings and the rumpled white dress, followed her.

The squaw turned from the path and, as she walked swiftly on, gave several low calls which to Anne sounded like the notes of a bird. The last call was answered, and a moment later Nakanit appeared beside them. For a long time they went on in silence, and at last the squaw stopped suddenly.

"Oh!" exclaimed Anne, for directly in front of them was a wigwam, so cunningly built in behind a growth of small spruce trees that unless one knew of its whereabouts it might be easily passed by. The Indian girl laughed at Anne's exclamation, and nodded at her in a friendly manner.

"Go in," said the squaw. "Did no woman give you food to eat on your journey?"

Anne shook her head.

"Umph!" grunted the squaw, and turned toward Nakanit, evidently telling her to bring Anne something to eat.

The Indian girl opened a basket that stood near the wigwam door and took out some thin cakes made of corn meal, and handed them to Anne. Anne ate them hungrily; they tasted very sweet and good, and, when she had eaten the last one, she turned toward the squaw who sat beside her, and said, "Thank you very much. The cakes were good."

The squaw nodded gravely. Anne looked round the wigwam with curious eyes. It was evident that Nakanit and her mother were nearly ready for a journey. The two baskets were near the door, the roll of blankets beside them, well tied up with stout thongs of deerskin, and the little brush wigwam had nothing else in it.

The Indian girl stood with her dark eyes fixed on Anne, and the squaw talked rapidly for a few moments, evidently giving the girl information or directions; then she lifted the smaller of the two baskets, and fastened its deerskin strap over Nakanit's shoulders. The roll of blankets and the other basket she carried herself.

"Follow," she said to Anne; "we journey toward Wellfleet and you can go with us."

Anne's face brightened, and she began to feel that her troubles were over. She picked up her own bundle and followed the squaw and the Indian girl out through the woods and across a meadow where a few cattle were feeding.

"This must be Truro," Anne thought to herself as she trudged silently on beside her new friends.

It grew very warm and there was no shade, and Anne began to feel tired, but neither Nakanit nor her mother seemed to notice the heat. It was past noon before they made any stop, and as Anne, who was some distance behind her companions, saw the squaw turn toward a little wooded hill and begin to lower the basket from her shoulders, she gave a long tired sigh of relief. Nakanit heard and turned toward her, and reached out her free hand to take Anne's bundle. But Anne shook her head, and tightened her hold on it. This seemed to anger the Indian girl, and with a surly word she gave Anne a push, sending her over into a clump of wild rose bushes. As Anne reached out to save herself the thorns scratched her hands and arms and she cried out. The squaw turned, and, as she had not seen the push, thought that Anne had stumbled, and began to laugh at her and to mock her cries. This delighted Nakanit, who joined in so loudly that Anne stopped in terrified amazement, and scrambled out as well as she could. Her feet ached, and she could hardly walk, but she went on behind Nakanit into the pleasant shade of the woods, and here her companions set down their baskets, and threw themselves down to rest. Anne looked at them a little fearfully; they had not spoken one word to her since leaving the wigwam.

The squaw opened the basket and gave each of the girls some of the corn bread, which they devoured hungrily. "There are berries over there," she said briefly, pointing toward the slope, "and water."

Nakanit was already running toward the slope, but Anne did not move; she was still hungry and very thirsty, but too tired to walk, and as she lay on the soft grass she began to dread the moment when the squaw might start on again. It was not long before Nakanit returned. She brought with her a cunningly made basket of oak leaves pinned together with twigs, and heaped full of blueberries; the squaw shook her head as Nakanit offered her the berries, and pointed toward Anne. Nakanit obeyed, but somewhat sulkily, for she had meant to help Anne with the bundle, and was still angry at Anne's refusal.

"How good they taste," exclaimed Anne as she helped herself to a handful, and she smiled up gratefully at Nakanit. The Indian girl's face brightened, and she smiled back, and sitting down beside Anne held the basket forward for her to take more. When the berries were finished Nakanit again disappeared.

After several hours' rest the squaw started on again, and Anne followed after wondering where Nakanit was. In a short time they came down to a sandy beach.

"Why, look! There's Nakanit!" exclaimed Anne, pointing toward the water, where a bark canoe floated near the shore with Nakanit in it, holding her paddle ready to send the craft to whatever point on the beach her mother might direct.

The squaw called, and with a twist of the paddle the girl sent the canoe to the shore. The squaw lifted in the baskets, the roll of blankets and Anne's bundle. "Sit there, and be quiet," she said, and Anne stepped in very carefully and sat down on the bottom of the canoe.

It was now late in the afternoon. The water was very calm, and as Nakanit and her mother dipped their paddles and sent the canoe swiftly along, Anne looked back toward the wooded shore and was very glad that she was not plodding along over the fields and hills. It was much cooler on the water, and the little girl wondered if her Aunt Martha missed her at all. "But perhaps she is glad that I ran away," thought Anne, for she was sure that she had not given either Amanda or Mrs. Stoddard any reason to be unkind or to blame her. "Rose Freeman will be glad I came; I know she will," was her comforting thought.

The Indians did not speak save for an occasional word of direction from the squaw. The sun had set when they turned the canoe toward the shore. Nakanit pulled the canoe up on the sand beyond reach of the tide, and the squaw led the way to a little opening among the trees, and there Anne was surprised to

"SIT THERE AND BE QUIET"

find another wigwam, very much like the one they had left that morning. The squaw spread the blankets, gave the girls the corn cakes with strips of dried fish for their supper, and they had water from a near-by brook.

Anne was soon fast asleep, quite forgetful of her strange surroundings and of the friends in Province Town.

Meanwhile those friends had now nearly given up the hope of finding her.

Amanda Cary's jealousy had vanished the moment she heard of Anne's disappearance.

"I do not know what I shall do with the child," Mrs. Cary said anxiously, when Amanda cried herself to sleep on the night after Anne left home, and when, on the next morning, she began sobbing bitterly at the mention of her playmate's name.

"Amanda's ashamed; that's what's the matter with her," declared Amos boldly.

Amanda's sobs stopped, and she looked at her brother with startled eyes. What would become of her, she wondered, if the Stoddards should ever find out that she, Amanda, was the one to blame; that Anne had not deserved any punishment.

"Amos, don't plague your sister," said Mrs. Cary. "You know she loves Anne, even if the girl did slap her. Amanda has a good heart, and she does not hold resentment," and Mrs. Cary looked at Amanda with loving eyes.

At her mother's words Amanda began to cry again. She thought to herself that she could never tell the truth, never. "Everybody will hate me if I do," she thought, and then, remembering Anne and hearing her father say on the second day after her disappearance that there was now little hope of finding the runaway, she felt that she must tell Mrs. Stoddard.

"I'll wager I could find Anne," said Amos as he and Amanda sat on the door-step. "She's started for Brewster."

"Oh, Amos!" Amanda's voice was full of delight. "I shouldn't wonder if she had."

"But Captain Stoddard says he followed the Truro path and no sign of her; and other people say that wolves would get her if she started to walk."

Amanda's face had brightened at Amos's assertion that he knew he could find Anne, and now she asked eagerly:

"What makes you think you could find her, Amos?"

"You won't tell?" and Amos looked at his sister sharply.

"I promise, hope to die, I won't," answered Amanda.

"Well, I'll tell you. I think she started for Truro, and will go by the meadows and over the hill instead of the regular path. I know the way I'd go, and I know I could find her; but father just shakes his head and won't let me try."

"Amos, you go," said Amanda. "Promise you'll go. I'll tell you something if you won't ever tell. It's something awful!"

"I won't tell," said the boy.

"I made Anne run away! Yes, I did. I was angry when she told me about going to Boston again, and going in a chaise, and I pushed her—"

"And then you came home and told mother that yarn!" interrupted Amos; "and mother went and told Mrs. Stoddard, and so Anne got punished and didn't know what for. You're a nice sister to have!" and the boy's face expressed his disgust.

"But, Amos, I didn't s'pose Anne would run away," pleaded Amanda.

"Hmph!" muttered Amos. "Well, she has, and whatever happens to her will be your fault."

"O-ooh—dear," wailed the little girl. "What shall I do?"

"Nothing," answered Amos relentlessly; "only of course now I've got to find her."

"And you won't ever tell about me," pleaded Amanda.

"I'd be ashamed to let anybody know I had a sister like you," answered Amos.

"Amos, you're real good," responded Amanda, somewhat to her brother's surprise. "When will you start?"

"Right off," declared the boy. "I'll put a jug of water and something to eat in my boat, and I'll go round to

Truro—Anne must have got that far—and I'll keep on until I find her and tell her how ashamed I am of you."

"And say I'm sorry, Amos; promise to tell her I'm sorry," pleaded Amanda.

"Lots of use being sorry," said the boy. "When they miss me you can tell them just where I've gone and that I'll be home Saturday night, anyway, or let them hear from me if I don't come."

"I do believe you'll find her, Amos," declared Amanda.

"Sure!" answered the boy.

CHAPTER IV

WITH THE MASHPEES

AMOS was so frequently in his boat that no one gave any especial attention when they saw him push off from shore and row steadily in the direction of Truro. He was not missed at home until supper time; then, as the little family gathered around the table, Mrs. Cary said:

" 'Tis time Amos was here. He's not often late for his supper."

"He won't be here for supper," announced Amanda; "he's gone to find Anne!"

"My soul!" exclaimed Mrs. Cary; "gone to find Anne, indeed. What possesses the children of this settlement is more than I can answer. And you, Amanda! Here you are all smiles and twinkles, as if you thought it a great thing for your brother to start off like this."

"He's gone by boat, I vow," said Mr. Cary.

"Yes, he means to row to Truro, and catch up with Anne. And he said to tell you he'd be back, or get you news of him in some way, by Saturday," and Amanda nodded smilingly, as if she were quite sure that her father and mother would be quite satisfied with Amos now that she had given them his message.

"Amos shall have his way in one thing," said Mr. Cary. "As soon as he is back, aye, if he comes Saturday or not, I'll put him aboard the first craft that can get out of harbor, and the farther her port the better. A year on shipboard is what the boy needs."

"You wouldn't send the boy with a strange captain?" Mrs. Cary questioned anxiously.

"Indeed I will. So long as he's on board a ship we shall know where he is," declared Amos's father. "We can do nothing now but wait. Find Anne, indeed! who knows where to look for the poor child?"

"Amos knows," said Amanda.

But Mr. and Mrs. Cary shook their heads. They did not feel much anxiety as to Amos's safety, for the boys of the settlement were used to depending on themselves, and many boys no older than Amos Cary or Jimmie Starkweather had made a voyage to the West Indies, or to some far southern port; but they were displeased that he should have started off without permission.

Saturday came, but Amos did not appear, but toward evening a Truro man brought Mr. Cary word that Amos had been in Truro, and had started for Brewster that morning.

"He's a sailor, that boy!" declared the Truro man admiringly. "He hoisted that square foot of sail-cloth, and went out of harbor at sunrise with a fair wind. He said he had 'business in Brewster,'" and the Truro man laughed good-naturedly. "But he's a smart boy," he added.

Mr. Cary made no answer, but his stern face softened a little at the praise of Amos. Nevertheless he was firmly resolved that Amos should be sent on a long voyage. "The harder master he has the better," thought the father. "I'm too easy with him."

When Amos hoisted his "square foot of sail" and headed for Wellfleet, he saw a canoe some distance ahead of him.

"Two squaws paddling and one doing nothing," thought the boy. "Wonder where they're bound?" But it was no unusual sight to see Indian canoes in those waters, and Amos did not think much about it. But his course brought him nearer and nearer to the graceful craft, and all at once he noticed that the figure sitting in the canoe was a little white girl. At that very moment Anne turned her face toward him.

"Amos!" she exclaimed, springing to her feet.

There was an angry exclamation from the squaw, a yell from Nakanit, and in an instant the girls and woman were in the water. Anne's jump had upset the delicately balanced craft. The baskets bobbed and floated on the water. Anne's bundle was not to be seen, while Anne herself, clutching at the slippery side of the canoe called "Amos! Amos!" in a terrified voice.

But it was no new experience for either the squaw or Nakanit. In a moment Anne felt a strong grasp on her shoulder. "Keep quiet," commanded the squaw. "Let go the canoe." As Anne obeyed she saw Nakanit close beside her, and, while the squaw kept her firm grasp on Anne's shoulder, the girl righted the canoe, and easily and surely regained her place in it. The squaw lifted Anne in, and quickly followed her. Amos had brought his boat as near as possible and now rescued the baskets and floating paddles, and handed them to Nakanit.

The squaw scowled at Anne, and when the girl bewailed her lost bundle muttered angrily.

"Want to get in my boat, Anne?" asked the boy.

Before Anne could answer the squaw with a strong sweep of her paddle had sent the canoe some distance from the boat, while Nakanit called back some word to Amos, evidently of warning not to follow them. But Anne turned her head and called "Amos! Amos!" For the scowling faces of her companions frightened her, and she wished herself safely in Amos's boat.

The breeze had now died away, and Amos was soon left some distance behind. Anne did not dare turn her head to see if he were following the canoe, which was now moving ahead rapidly as the Indians swiftly wielded their paddles.

"Go to Brewster," announced the squaw after a little silence.

Anne, huddled up in her wet clothes, frightened and unhappy, nodded her head in answer. Then, remembering that the squaw had bidden her to sit still, and that her jump had upset the canoe, she ventured to say: "I'm sorry I jumped."

The squaw's scowl disappeared, and she gave a grunt of approval, and then, evidently, repeated Anne's words to Nakanit, for the Indian girl smiled and nodded. Anne began to realize that they were really kind and good-natured, and that she had no reason to be afraid.

"I was surprised to see Amos," she continued.

The squaw nodded again, and repeated, "Go to Brewster."

Anne could now hear the sound of the oars, and knew that Amos was rowing toward them. The paddles began to move more swiftly, and the sound of the oars grew more indistinct. Anne realized that Amos could not keep up with the canoe. But she was sure that he would follow them, and it made her feel less uneasy.

"Amos is a good boy," she explained to the squaw, but there was no response. "I'd like to tell him that you've been good to me," continued Anne.

At this the squaw, with a word to Nakanit, held her paddle motionless, and very soon Amos was close beside them.

"Tell him," commanded the squaw.

So Anne told her little story of adventure, and said, "And they are going to take me right to Rose Freeman in Brewster. Nakanit's mother talks English."

Amos listened in amazement. "I told Amanda you'd started for Brewster," he responded, "and I sent word to father that I was going there, so I might as well go. I've got things to eat. Amanda's sorry," he added, looking rather ashamed as he spoke his sister's name.

The squaw now dipped her paddle again, and the canoe and boat moved forward. Anne began to think about her lost bundle, and to remember how neatly Rose Freeman dressed. "She will be ashamed of me," thought the girl, looking down at her wet and faded skirt and bare feet.

"Say, don't we stop anywhere for dinner?" asked Amos. "It's getting hot work rowing all this time."

The squaw looked at the boy sharply, and then turned the canoe toward the shore. They landed on a beach, close by the mouth of a stream of clear water. A little way from the beach they found shade under a branching oak-tree.

"I'll build a fire," suggested Amos, "and I'll get some clams; shall I?" and he turned toward the squaw.

She nodded, and seemed rather surprised when she saw that the boy understood her own way of getting fire, and when he asked for a basket and soon returned with it well filled with clams, which he roasted in the hot sand under the coals, she evidently began to think well of him. Amos shared his bread and a piece of cold beef which he had brought from home with his companions, and, with a quantity of blueberries that Nakanit had gathered while Amos roasted the clams, they all had enough to eat, and Amos said everything tasted better than if eaten in the house, at which the squaw nodded and smiled.

Anne found a chance to whisper to Amos: "Don't tell her I ran away."

"All right, but I fear she knows it," replied the boy.

It was in the early evening when the canoe, closely followed by Amos's rowboat, left Wellfleet harbor behind them and headed for Brewster. The squaw had decided that it would be easier to go on than to wait for another day, and Anne and Amos were glad to go on as soon as possible.

At first Amos had wondered why the squaw had promised to take Anne to Brewster, and had decided that probably the Indians were bound in that direction when they fell in with Anne. This was really one reason, but it was Anne's mention of the name of Freeman that had made the squaw willing to do the girl a service. For the Freemans of Brewster had been good friends to the Mashpee Indians, and the squaw felt bound to help any friend of theirs.

She had questioned Amos sharply as to his reason for following Anne, and Amos had told her the truth: that his sister had not treated Anne fairly, so that Anne had been punished, and had run away. "So, of course," added the boy, "I had to come after her and be sure that she was all right."

The squaw understood, and evidently thought well of Amos for his undertaking. Anne felt much happier to know that a friend was close at hand, and that Amos on his return home would tell her Aunt Martha Stoddard that she was safely in Brewster. But the lost bundle troubled her a good deal. As she sat in the swiftly moving canoe and watched the steady dip of the paddles she thought that the Indians had been very good to her. "If I had my bundle now I would give Nakanit the cape and the beads; indeed I would," she said to herself.

The midsummer moon shone down upon the beautiful harbor. Every wooded point or sloping field was plainly outlined in the clear water, and there was the pleasant fragrance of pine and bayberry mingled with the soft sea air. It was much pleasanter than journeying in the sun. The squaw and Nakanit began to sing, and although neither Anne nor Amos understood the words, they were both sure that the musical notes told of birds flying over moonlit water.

It was midnight when the squaw turned the canoe toward shore. It proved to be the mouth of a small inlet up which they went for some distance, Amos keeping close behind.

"Look, Anne!" he exclaimed as the Indians stopped paddling. "There is a camp-fire. I do believe it's the Mashpee village."

"Sshh," warned the squaw in a sharp voice. At the sound of the boy's voice a number of dark figures appeared to spring up from the ground, and the squaw called out a word of greeting. A moment later she was talking rapidly to several tall figures who came to meet her, evidently telling Anne's story and that of Amos.

Anne could distinguish the word "Freeman" in the squaw's talk.

Amos pulled his boat up on shore, and stood wondering what would happen next. He looked toward the wigwams and the smoldering camp-fires, and almost forgave Amanda, because his journey was bringing him into the Mashpee village.

One of the Indians gave him a little push, and pointed toward a wigwam. It was evident that the squaw was the only one who spoke English.

"Go with him," she said to Amos.

"All right," responded the boy; "here's your bundle, Anne," he said, holding it out toward her. "I fished it out of the water when you tipped over. Guess it isn't much wet."

Anne was almost too delighted to speak. She hugged the bundle in her arms and followed Nakanit up the path toward the village. This was evidently the squaw's home, and her wigwam had many deerskins, blankets and baskets.

Nakanit led Anne toward the back of the wigwam where lay a pile of spruce boughs over which deerskins were thrown. In a few moments the Indian girl and Anne lay on this rude couch fast asleep.

When Anne awoke the next morning there was no one in the wigwam. Everything seemed very quiet.

Anne's first thought was for her beloved bundle that she had carefully set down beside her bed. It was not there. The little girl slid to her feet, and began looking about the wigwam. There was no trace of it. Anne began to feel very unhappy. It had been hard to make up her mind to give Nakanit her treasured corals and her pretty cape, but it was even harder to bear to have them disappear like this. She threw herself back on the bed and began to cry bitterly. She wished that Rose Freeman had never thought of asking her to come to Brewster, and that she was safe in Province Town with Aunt Martha.

She stopped crying suddenly, for she felt a hand smoothing her hair, and she looked up to find Nakanit sitting beside her, and at her feet rested the bundle. It was plain that the mischievous Indian girl had wished to tease the little white girl, but had relented at the sight of her tears.

"Oh," exclaimed Anne, "I'm so glad!" and she began to unfasten the bundle, spreading out the blue cape and muslin dress, and laying "Martha Stoddard" down on the deerskins. Then she took up the string of coral beads and turning toward Nakanit fastened them around her neck. "I want to give you these for being good to me," she said. The Indian girl understood the gift if not the words, and was evidently delighted. Hearing a noise at the entrance they looked up to see the squaw smiling in at them. She had heard Anne's words, and now came toward the girls. Anne picked up her blue cape and held it out toward the squaw. "I wish I had something better to give you," she said.

The squaw took it eagerly, and with a grunt of satisfaction, and then, turning to Nakanit, began chattering rapidly. Nakanit ran toward a big basket in the corner and came back with several pairs of soft moccasins. Kneeling before Anne she tried them on her feet until a pair was found that fitted.

"Now go with Nakanit to the lake," said the squaw, and Anne followed Nakanit out of the wigwam through the woods to a clear little lake where the girls bathed, braided their hair, and then came back to eat heartily of the simple food the squaw gave them.

CHAPTER V

AT BREWSTER

"Look, look, Aunt Hetty. Here are some Indians coming up the path, and I do believe that they have a little white boy and girl with them," and Rose Freeman drew her aunt to the open window that looked down over a smooth green lawn to an elm-shaded village street.

Aunt Hetty's well-starched dress rustled pleasantly as she hurried to join Rose.

"It's old Nakanit and her daughter," she said. "My mother taught her a good deal, and she often comes to see me. Those are surely white children. I wonder what the trouble is. Old Nakanit knows that the Sabbath is not a day for idle visits, and indeed, Rose, it does not become us to be stretching our heads out of the window. There, they are on the porch now. Why, Rose!" For with a quick exclamation the girl had run from the room and when Mrs. Freeman followed she found her with an arm about a little moccasined dark-eyed girl, saying, "Why, it is Anne; it is dear little Anne Nelson."

"I declare!" exclaimed Mrs. Freeman. "And did you fetch the child, Nakanit? Sit down and I will have Hepsibah bring you some cool milk and cake."

Nakanit grunted appreciatively, and while the Indians were eating Anne told Rose all the story of her journey.

"I do not know why Aunt Martha shut me up and said that I could not visit you, Rose," said Anne; "if I had been disobedient or careless I do not know it."

Amos listened, looking very flushed and unhappy, for he knew that it was Amanda's story that had caused Anne's punishment and made her a runaway. But he had promised his sister that he would not betray her, and now that Anne had reached Brewster in safety he resolved to keep silent. "But Amanda shall tell Mrs. Stoddard; indeed she shall," the boy said to himself.

The Indians soon rose from the porch steps to depart, and as Anne said good-bye to them she felt that she was parting from friends, and tried to tell them so.

"And you are going home to Province Town, and will tell Aunt Martha that I am safe," she said to Amos. "You were real good to come after me, Amos, and you tell Amanda not to be sorry she slapped me; that it's all right."

Amos wriggled about uneasily at Anne's message. He was almost resolved not to go home at all.

"I reckon I'll stay with the Mashpees a while," he answered. "There's an Indian boy who talks English and he's told me lots of things: how to set traps for foxes and woodchucks, and how to make fish-spears, and he can stay under water longer than I can. He's fine. You ought to hear him tell stories. Last night he told me of a tribe of Indians who sent six of their bravest warriors out to sea in a canoe, without food or paddles, so as to prove to other tribes that their braves could not be harmed anywhere. And they were carried by the winds and waves to a wonderful island where there were friendly Indians; and they hunted wild deer, and made bows and arrows, and paddles, and caught wild birds, and when another summer came back they came to Cape Cod with many canoes, and skins, and much deer-meat, so that their tribe made them all great chiefs. And this boy who told me is one of the descendants of the very bravest chief, and he wants me to stay and be his brother," and Amos looked as if he would like nothing better than to be adopted into the Mashpee tribe.

"What's the Indian boy's name?" questioned Anne.

"I don't think much of his name," said Amos, a little regretfully; "it's 'Shining Fish.'"

"But you won't stay with the Indians, Amos, will you?" pleaded Anne.

"I s'pose I'll have to go home," agreed Amos. "I wonder what Jimmie Starkweather will say when I tell him about living with Indians," and Amos looked more cheerful at the thought of Jimmie's surprise and envy when he should describe his adventures. "Nothing ever happens to Jimmie," he added, in a satisfied tone.

After Amos and the Indians had started on their way back to the Indian village Rose and Anne followed Mrs. Freeman into the square comfortable house. Mrs. Freeman had heard all about Anne, and now, as she noticed the torn and soiled dress, the untidy hair and moccasin-covered feet, she whispered to Rose: "Take the child right up-stairs. I don't want your uncle to see her looking so like a wild child of the woods."

Rose nodded laughingly. Aunt Hetty Freeman was known as one of the best housekeepers in Brewster, and no one had ever seen her looking other than "spick and span," as her husband often admiringly declared. Rose always said that she could tell just what part of the big house Aunt Hetty was in because she could hear her starched skirts rattle; and she realized that Anne's untidy appearance was a real trouble to her kind-hearted aunt.

Anne looked at the broad stairway admiringly, and exclaimed at the sight of a tall clock on the landing. "It's better than Boston, isn't it, Rose?" she said, as Rose took her into the big comfortable room, with its high, curtained bed and chintz curtained windows.

"It's a dear house," answered the older girl, who was too loyal to her home to think any other place quite as good. "You are the bravest child I ever heard of," Rose continued admiringly, drawing Anne down beside her on the broad cushioned window-seat; "to think of your starting out to come all the way alone to Brewster through the wilderness!"

"I guess I should have been lost but for the Indians," replied Anne; "but when Aunt Martha said I could not come, that she did not want to hear more of any visit to Brewster or Boston, I had to run away. But now I'm sorry," and Anne began to cry bitterly. Rose, too, looked very unhappy, for she realized that Captain and Mrs. Stoddard would be greatly troubled until they knew of the little girl's safety. And, besides that, she was sure that her father would not be willing to take a runaway child to Boston. But Rose resolved not to worry about it, and not to tell Anne that she feared that she would be sent home to her Aunt Martha, instead of taking the wonderful journey to Boston.

So she comforted her little guest, and told her not to feel bad—that Aunt Martha and Uncle Enos would be only too happy to know that she was safe.

"And you can wear your moccasins these hot days," continued Rose, "and you will look very nice indeed."

Anne was soon dressed in the neat clothing, and, with her hair brushed and smoothly braided, she looked like quite a different child from the little girl who had journeyed with Nakanit.

"I am glad to look nice to go to Boston," Anne said soberly, as they went down the stairs.

"Oh, dear!" thought the older girl; "how can I tell the poor child that I am almost sure that father will find a way to send her safely back to Province Town?"

Rose's father and uncle spoke kindly to Anne as she came into the sitting-room, and Aunt Hetty's skirts rustled briskly as she moved about the room, and then she went out in the shed and came back with a round, low basket in which lay two black kittens, which she placed in Anne's lap saying: "There, little girls and little kittens always like each other; so you can have Pert and Prim for your own while you stay with us."

"Oh, thank you," said Anne delightedly, for the two little kittens began to purr happily as she smoothed their soft fur.

Rose found an opportunity to tell her father all about Anne's reason for running away.

"She did not know why her Aunt Martha shut her up," pleaded Rose.

But Mr. Freeman shook his head soberly. "We'll have to send her home by the first chance to Province Town," he answered, and Rose went back to her little friend feeling that all her pleasant plans for Anne's visit must come to an end.

"But she shall have a good time here in Brewster," resolved the girl.

"Shall we start for Boston on Tuesday or Thursday?" Anne asked the next morning, as she helped Rose put their pleasant chamber in order.

"Father has not decided," replied Rose, feeling rather cowardly that she did not tell Anne the truth.

"It will be fine to ride in a chaise," went on Anne happily, "and to stop in taverns, and see towns along the way. Your father is indeed good, Rose, to take me."

"We must do up the dishes for Aunt Hetty," said Rose briskly, "and then we can walk down the street, and maybe father will drive us about the town."

While the girls were busy helping Aunt Hetty, Rose's father was on his way to the Mashpee village to see Amos Cary and to give him a letter to take to Captain Stoddard. He found the boy just ready to start. Shining Fish had launched his canoe and was to go part of the way with his new friend, greatly to Amos's delight.

"Anne wasn't to blame." Amos repeated this a number of times so earnestly that Mr. Freeman began to realize that the boy knew more than he was willing to tell, and to blame Amos.

"That Amanda," Amos whispered to himself, as he blushed and stammered and evaded Mr. Freeman's questions.

"I suppose I can trust you with this letter to Captain Stoddard?" said Mr. Freeman.

Amos lifted his head, and his blue eyes did not falter in meeting the stern look of the man.

"I'll give it to him," he replied, and Mr. Freeman felt quite sure that the letter would reach its destination.

When Amos's boat drew near the landing at Province Town, he saw that his father, Amanda, and the Stoddards were all waiting for him. He felt himself to be almost like the chiefs of whom Shining Fish had told him, and quite expected to be praised and made much of; but as he sprang ashore he felt his father's hand on his shoulder.

"March yourself straight to the house, young man. I'll see that you pay for this fool's errand," said Mr. Cary.

Amos wriggled away from his father's grasp. "I've got a letter for Captain Enos. Anne's in Brewster," he announced.

"Thank heaven!" exclaimed Mrs. Stoddard. "And did you find her, Amos? You are a brave boy! Why, Mr. Cary, there's not another boy in the village who thought of Anne's going to Brewster, or man either for that matter," and Mrs. Stoddard patted the boy's shoulder affectionately, while Mr. Cary regarded Amos with puzzled eyes, hardly knowing whether to blame or praise him.

While Captain Enos read the letter Amos briefly told the story of his adventures to the little group, saving all that Shining Fish had told him to relate to Jimmy Starkweather as soon as opportunity should occur.

"Well, go home to your mother," said Mr. Cary in a more gentle voice, and Amanda kept close beside her brother as they turned toward home.

"You've got to tell Mrs. Stoddard," said Amos. "Yes, you have," he went on, almost fiercely, as Amanda began to whimper. "Everybody's blaming Anne, and it's not fair; you've got to tell."

Amanda stopped short and looked at her brother accusingly. "You promised not to tell," she said.

"Well, I haven't," answered the boy, "and I won't. I'm ashamed to, beside the promise. Anne said, when I told her that you said you were sorry, that I was to tell you 'twas all right. She seemed to feel bad because you were sorry."

"Well, Amos Cary, I won't tell Mrs. Stoddard; so now!" declared Amanda angrily. "Anne is all right, and going to Boston in a chaise. You ought to be satisfied. Let them think what they want to, I don't care. And you've got to go to sea. Father's told Captain Nash that he can have you, and the 'Sea Gull' sails next week."

"Truly, Amanda! Say, that's great news. I do believe I'm the luckiest boy on the Cape. Are you sure, Amanda?" Amos's eyes were shining, his shoulders had straightened themselves, and, for the moment, he quite forgot everything except the wonderful news.

"Do you want to go?" and Amanda's voice was full of disappointment.

"Want to! Why, the 'Sea Gull' is bound for the West Indies her next voyage, and maybe the English will try and catch us," and Amos's voice expressed his delight. "Are you sure, Amanda?" he questioned eagerly, and turned toward his sister in surprise, for Amanda was crying. It seemed to the unhappy child that everything was going wrong. She did not want Amos to go away, and she had hoped that he would persuade his father to let him remain at home, and here he was rejoicing and triumphant. She was in great fear that Anne would tell the Stoddards the truth, and then Amanda hardly knew what might befall her. She wished that she was a boy and could go with Amos in the "Sea Gull."

"It is indeed good news to know that our little girl is safe in Brewster," said Mrs. Stoddard, as she read Mr. Freeman's letter, "but what shall we do, Enos, about bringing her home? Mr. Freeman truly says that, while Rose is eager to take Anne to Boston, we may feel that it would not be right for her to go. It is indeed a puzzle, is it not? Whatever possessed Anne to turn upon Amanda in such fashion, and then to run off?" and the good woman shook her head dolefully.

"I'll have to sail to Brewster and fetch her home," responded the captain, but his face was very sober. He would have been glad if the Freemans had written that they would take Anne to Boston, for he did not want the child disappointed.

"Well, well, we'll let her see how glad we are to have her safe home, shall we not, Enos? I'll say no more to her about her naughtiness, and I am sure Mrs. Cary will tell Amanda to forgive Anne and be friends again, and all will go on pleasantly," but they both felt sorry that it seemed best for the little girl whom they so dearly loved to have to give up the wonderful journey up the Cape to Boston in the Freemans' fine chaise.

CHAPTER VI

AMANDA'S CONSCIENCE

Amos Cary and Jimmy Starkweather lay on the warm sand in the narrow shadow cast by a fishing dory pulled up on the beach. No chief returning from far-off islands could have been more a hero than was Amos among the boys and girls of the settlement. They followed him about, and listened eagerly to all that he had to tell them of the Indians. Then, too, he was to go in the "Sea Gull" with Captain Nash, the swiftest schooner and the smartest captain sailing out of the harbor, and Jimmie Starkweather felt that Amos was having greater good fortune than any boy could hope for.

"Maybe the 'Sea Gull' can't get out of port," said Jimmie, digging his bare toes in the soft sand. "The English ships keep a sharp outlook for a schooner loaded down with salt fish. I'll bet Captain Nash won't get beyond Chatham."

"Pooh!" responded Amos scornfully. "We can sail right away from their old tubs. But 'twill be great if they do follow us."

" 'Twould be just your good fortune," said Jimmie. "I do wish my father would let me go with you, Amos. Who knows what adventures you may have!"

For a few moments the two boys did not speak; they lay looking out over the beautiful harbor, and their minds were full of vague hopes of adventure. Jimmie was the first to break the silence.

"You won't see Shining Fish again, will you, Amos?"

"No; did I show you what he gave me?" And Amos pulled out a stout deerskin thong from inside his flannel blouse. The claw of a bird was fastened to the thong. "See! It's a hawk's claw," exclaimed Amos; "and as long as I wear it no enemy can touch me. I gave Shining Fish my jack-knife," continued Amos. "You'd like him, Jimmie; he knew stories about chiefs and warriors, and he had killed a fox with his bow and arrow. He told me about a chief of their tribe who lived long ago and was the strongest man that ever lived. He used to go on long journeys, way beyond Cape Cod, with his band of warriors, and once he met an unfriendly tribe, and they laughed when the braves told how strong their chief was. 'Can he conquer a wild bull?' one of them asked, and the brave answered, 'Aye, or two wild bulls.'

"So the unfriendly Indians laughed louder, and were glad, for they thought they could destroy the chief even without a battle. Well, they arranged that this brave chief was to go alone into a fenced-in place and meet two wild bulls, and if he conquered them the unfriendly tribe would own him the strongest chief in the world, and would be subject to him. It was great, Jimmie, to hear Shining Fish tell it. He said the great chief marched into the place where the bulls were, and they came dashing toward him, and their hoofs rang upon the ground, and their nostrils sent out sheets of flame, but the chief never flinched a step, and the bulls stopped short and trembled. Then the chief sprang upon the nearest, and seized him by the horns, and they wrestled until the bull fell to its knees tired out. Then he grabbed at the other, and threw it, and all the Indians began to wonder how any chief could be so strong."

"S'pose it's true?" questioned Jimmie.

"Sure!" answered Amos. "What's Captain Stoddard doing to his boat?" he continued. Captain Enos was evidently not bound out on a fishing trip, for he was making his boat as tidy as possible.

"He's going to sail over to Brewster to fetch Anne back," answered Jimmie.

"But Anne is going to Boston with Rose Freeman," said Amos.

Jimmie shook his head. "No, the Freemans won't take her because she ran away," he explained, and looked up in amazement, for Amos had sprung to his feet and was racing along the beach toward Captain Stoddard's boat as fast as his feet would carry him.

Jimmie laughed. "I'll bet Amos wants to go to Brewster," he decided.

Amos did not want to go to Brewster. But he had instantly resolved that Anne must not be stopped from going to Boston. Even as he ran he could see that there was no time to spare in reaching Captain Enos, for he was already pushing off from shore.

"Captain Enos! Captain Enos!" he called frantically, and the captain looked toward him. "Wait a minute! wait!" yelled the boy, and the captain waited, saying good-humoredly:

"Never saw such a boy as that one. He can't bear to see a boat put off unless he's in it."

"Captain Enos, you mustn't bring Anne back," said Amos as he ran out into the shallow water and grasped the side of the boat. "It wouldn't be fair; it wasn't her fault," he added.

"Whose fault was it?" asked the captain.

"Wait!" commanded Amos, remembering his promise to his sister. "Wait just ten minutes, Captain Enos, before you start. I'll be back," and away went Amos up the beach and along the sandy path to the house.

"Amos is going to come out first rate, I can see that plain enough," said Captain Enos, watching the boy's flying figure, and he was not surprised when he saw Amos coming back with Amanda held fast by the hand.

The boy and girl stopped at the edge of the water.

"Tell him, Amanda," commanded Amos.

"It's my fault," whimpered Amanda. "I got my mother to tell Mrs. Stoddard that Anne slapped me and ran off with the luncheon. And she didn't. I slapped her."

"Clear as mud," muttered the captain; then in a louder tone, "Amos, you're going to make a good American sailor, and we're all going to be proud of you. And I guess Amanda's going to do better after this," and he pushed off from shore.

"But you won't go to Brewster now!" called both the children.

"I'll have to. Must go and tell the Freemans that we're willing for Anne to go to Boston, and to tell Anne that her Aunt Martha knows the truth. You just run up and tell Mrs. Stoddard all about it, Amanda," he answered; and, having sent his boat into deep water, the captain drew in his oars and began hoisting the big mainsail.

For a few moments the boy and girl stood watching him. Then, with a long sigh, Amanda turned to go toward the Stoddard house. Amos began to feel a little sorry for her.

"Say, Amanda, I'll go tell her," he called.

"You mind your own business, Amos Cary," and Amanda turned toward him angrily. "I'll tell Mrs. Stoddard myself, and then I'll go home and tell my mother. I'll tell everybody, and when everybody hates and despises me I reckon you'll be satisfied," and without waiting for any response she went on up the path.

Amos turned and went back to the shade of the boat, but Jimmie Starkweather was no longer there. He wished more than ever that he was back with Shining Fish. Then he remembered that in another week he would be on board the "Sea Gull." He watched Captain Stoddard's sloop until it was only a white blur against the distant shore, and then went up the beach toward home.

Captain Enos had a favoring wind and a light heart, for he was glad to know that their little maid had not been to blame. "She ran away because she had not been fairly treated. 'Tis what older people sometimes do," he said to himself. "'Twas the very reason that sent our fathers out of England to America. I'll not fetch Anne back, for she called to me from the window and would have told me all the story had I been willing to listen," and then because his mind was at ease the captain began to sing an old song that he had learned as a boy. He had a musical voice, and the words drifted back pleasantly:

"A fit and fa-vor-able wind
    To further us provide;
And let it wait on us behind,
    Or lackey by our side;
From sudden gusts, from storms, from sands,
    And from the raging wave;
From shallows, rocks, and pirates' hands,
    Men, goods, and vessel save."

In Brewster time was going very smoothly with Anne. The Freemans were kind and pleasant people, and the big house was filled with many things of interest to a little girl. First of all there was black Hepsibah, a black woman whom Captain Freeman had brought, with her brother Josephus, from Cuba when they were small children. They had grown up in the Freeman household, and were valued friends and servants. Anne liked to hear Hepsibah laugh, and the negro woman's skirts were as stiffly starched as those of Mrs. Freeman herself, who had taught Hepsibah, and trained her to become an excellent housekeeper.

On the high mantelpiece in the dining-room were great branches of white coral, brought from the South Seas; on each side of the front door were huge pink shells. And in the funny little corner cupboard were delicately tinted pink cups and saucers, and the mahogany table was always set with a tall shining silver teapot, and a little fat pitcher and bowls of silver, and the plates were covered with red flowers and figures of queer people with sunshades. Rose told her that these plates came all the way from China, a country on the other side of the earth.

"When does your father say we shall start for Boston?" Anne asked, as the two girls walked down the shady pleasant street that led to the wharves. Anne was not a dull child, and she noticed that no word had been said of Boston, and began to wonder if Mr. Freeman blamed her for running away. "Perhaps your father thinks I am a wicked girl to have run away," she added before Rose could answer.

"Oh, Anne, no indeed; nobody would think you wicked," Rose answered promptly. "But father sent a letter to Captain Enos by Amos, and he expects that the captain will get word to us to-day or to-morrow—"

"To say whether I may go or not?" interrupted Anne. "Oh, Rose!" and there was a pleading note in the little girl's voice," I do want to go so much, and I do wonder and wonder why Amanda should have slapped me, and why Aunt Martha should have punished me. I do wish I could hear Aunt Martha say again that I was a good child, as she used often to do."

Rose clasped the little girl's hand affectionately. "I believe that Amanda was jealous because you were to have this visit," said Rose, "and who knows, perhaps by this time she is as sorry as can be, and has told Mrs. Stoddard all about it. Perhaps word may come this very night that your Aunt Martha thinks you are a good child, and forgives you for running away."

As the girls walked along they met a party of men carrying rifles, and hurrying toward Brewster Common.

"They are going to the training field," explained Rose, at Anne's surprised exclamation, "and may have to march to Boston to-morrow. Father is anxious to get home."

The wharves at Brewster were much larger and better cared for than the Province Town landing places; but there were few boats to be seen. Far out a sloop, coming briskly on before a favoring wind, attracted the girls' attention.

"Rose, that's the 'Morning Star,' Uncle Enos's sloop. I know it is," declared Anne; "and he will never let any one else sail her, so it's Uncle Enos! Let's hurry! He's coming straight for this very wharf."

The big sloop swung round, the mainsail came rattling down, and Captain Enos ran his craft skilfully up beside the long wharf just as Anne, closely followed by Rose, came running down the pier.

"Uncle Enos! Uncle Enos!" exclaimed Anne joyfully. "I'm so glad you've come," and she clasped both hands around his brawny arm as he stepped on the wharf. "And here is Rose," she continued as the elder girl stepped forward to speak to the captain.

"Growing more like a rose every day," declared Captain Enos, as he shook hands with Rose. "And here is our little maid all ready to start on the great journey, eh?" and he looked kindly down into Anne's smiling face. "And what would you girls say if I told you that I had sailed over here to take Anne back to Province Town?"

"Oh, Uncle Enos!"

"Oh, Captain Stoddard!" exclaimed the girls fearfully.

"Wouldn't like it, eh? Well," said the captain, "then we won't have it that way, and Anne may go with you."

"Oh, Uncle Enos!"

"Oh, Captain Stoddard!" The exclamations were the same, but the words were in such joyous tones that Captain Enos began to laugh heartily, as did Rose and Anne, so that it was a very merry party that went gaily up the street toward Mr. Freeman's house, where Captain Enos was warmly welcomed.

After supper he and Anne had a long talk together about Amanda and Amos. "Amanda's had a hard time, I reckon," declared the captain, "and if I know aught of her parents she will remember this all her life, and will not be so ready to bear false witness against her neighbor."

"I did not so much mind Amanda's slapping me," replied Anne soberly, "but I thought when Aunt Martha shut me up that 'twas because she no longer loved me."

"Tut, tut, and so you walked off into the wilderness. A very wrong thing to do, Anne," and Captain Enos's voice was very grave. "Your running away has made a sad talk in the settlement, and some of the people are ready to say that we have not treated you well, or you would not have fled from us."

Anne began to realize, for the first time, that she had acted very selfishly. Thinking of nothing but her wish to go to Boston with Rose she had made her best friends anxious and unhappy.

They were sitting on the broad sofa in the quiet sitting-room, and Anne leaned against Uncle Enos and said quickly: "I ought to go straight back to Province Town!" She said it in such a sharp voice that Uncle Enos looked at her wonderingly, and saw that tears were very near falling.

"No, Anne," he answered kindly. "I want you to go with the Freemans, and have a pleasant visit. Your father's ship will be in Boston in a few weeks, and he will rejoice to find you there and will bring you safely back to Province Town."

CHAPTER VII

THE BLACK-BEARDED MAN

ANNE and Rose Freeman stood at the gate all ready to enter the comfortable chaise with its broad seat and big wheels. The big brown horse was apparently eager to start, but black Josephus held him firmly until the girls and Mr. Freeman were seated, and then handed the reins to Mr. Freeman.

"Good-bye, good-bye," called the girls, leaning out beyond the hood of the chaise to wave to Aunt Hetty and Captain Freeman and Uncle Enos, who had stayed to see the travelers start on the ride to Boston.

"A horse is useful," remarked Uncle Enos, thoughtfully, as he watched them drive away, "but there's not one in Province Town settlement as yet. We have little need of one, with so many good boats."

The summer morning was clear and bright, and not too warm. They had made an early start, and the heavy dew still lingered on the trees and flowers.

"How far shall we go to-day, father?" asked Rose.

"We will pass the night in Sandwich, if all goes well," replied Mr. Freeman. "Your aunt has put us up a fine luncheon, and we will give Lady a rest toward noon and enjoy it."

The sandy roads made it rather slow traveling, but Anne was as happy as a bird. They got many glimpses of the sea, and now and then some wild creature would run across the road, or peer at them from the shelter of the woods. Once or twice a partridge, with her brood of little ones, fled before them, and there was a great deal for them to see and enjoy. Anne felt very happy to know that Aunt Martha and Uncle Enos had forgiven her for running away, and that they were glad for her to go to Boston. She did not cherish any ill-will against Amanda, and thought herself a very fortunate little girl to be sitting beside Rose Freeman and riding along the pleasant road in such a grand chaise.

Mr. Freeman told them that there was something very wonderful to be seen in Suet, a little village that they would pass through on their way to Sandwich. "Captain Sears is an old friend of mine," said Mr. Freeman, "and we will make him a call and he will be glad to show us how salt is made."

"Can he make salt?" questioned Anne.

"Yes, and a good thing for the colony it is; for salt is hard to get, with English frigates taking all the cargoes afloat," answered Mr. Freeman; "and Cape Cod is the very place to make it, for there is plenty of salt water." Then he told them how Captain Sears had first made long shallow troughs and filled them with the sea-water, and the sun dried up the water, leaving the salt in the bottom of the vats. "And now," continued Mr.

Freeman, "I hear he has had big kettles made, and with huge fires under them boils the water away and gets good salt in that fashion. We'll stop and have a look, if time allows."

Just before noon the sky began to grow dark, and there was a distant rumble of thunder. They were driving through a lonely stretch of country; there was no house in sight, and Mr. Freeman began to watch the sky with anxious eyes. He knew that, on the bare sandy plain over which they were now traveling, the wind would sweep with great force, sufficient perhaps to overturn the chaise. Rose and Anne grew very quiet as they heard the thunder and watched the threatening sky.

"We'll soon reach the Yarmouth woods," said Mr. Freeman encouragingly, "and if the storm comes may be able to find some sort of shelter, but I fear it will prevent our reaching the salt works."

Rose and Anne both thought to themselves that troughs and kettles filled with salt water would not be very much of a sight, and were very glad when the sandy plain was behind them and they were once more in the shelter of the woods, which broke the force of the wind. It was now raining in torrents.

"One good thing about this is that the rain will beat the sand down and make the traveling better," said Mr. Freeman.

The road was a mere lane, and they all began to feel a little uncomfortable and discouraged as the thunder deepened and came peal after peal, followed by shooting darts of lightning. The big horse was going at a good pace, but, all at once, Lady made a quick turn, and before Mr. Freeman could stop her had swung into an even more narrow track, half hidden by underbrush from the main road. In a few moments they saw a long low shingled house nearly hidden by closely growing trees.

"Well done, Lady!" exclaimed Mr. Freeman laughingly, as Lady stopped directly in front of the door.

Mr. Freeman handed the reins to Rose and sprang out, and rapped on the door, but no answer came.

"I don't believe there is any one here," he declared. "Stay in the chaise a moment, and I'll find out." As he spoke he gave the door a little push when, much to his surprise, it swung open and Mr. Freeman found himself face to face with a tall, black-bearded man who regarded him with a scowling countenance.

"What do you want?" he asked gruffly.

At that moment a peal of thunder heavier than any preceding it made Rose and Anne shrink more closely together in the corner of the chaise. "He looks like a pirate," whispered Rose fearfully.

"We want shelter until this storm is over," Mr. Freeman replied. "May I drive my horse into that shed?"

The man grunted an unwilling assent, and Mr. Freeman sprang back into the chaise and drove Lady under a rough shelter in the rear of the house.

"Don't go in the house, will you, father?" whispered Rose; for the man had opened a back door leading into the shed and was regarding his undesired guests with suspicious eyes.

"How did you happen to come here?" he asked gruffly. "This road don't lead nowheres."

"My horse turned in from the main road very suddenly," explained Mr. Freeman. "We had no plan except to get on to Sandwich as fast as possible."

"Going far?" questioned the man.

"We are on our way to Boston," answered Mr. Freeman.

"Guess the English are going to give the Yankees a lesson even if they couldn't hold Boston!" said the man with a smile, as if he would be glad to know his words would come true.

"I think not, sir," answered Mr. Freeman sharply; "and a Cape Cod man ought to be the last to say such a thing."

"You're not a Tory, then?" exclaimed the man eagerly. "Get right out of that chaise and come in. These your girls? Let me help you out, missy," and he came toward the carriage.

"Get out, Anne," said Mr. Freeman in a low tone, and in a moment the two girls were following the black-bearded man into a low dark kitchen.

"You folks looked so dressed up I thought like as not you were Tories," declared the man, as if wishing to explain his rude reception. "Now take seats, and I'll put your horse where it can have a bit of fodder."

Mr. Freeman followed the man back to the shed, and Anne and Rose looked at each other, and then glanced about the low dark room.

"I don't believe he's a pirate," whispered Anne; "anyway I'm glad to be in out of this dreadful storm."

"So am I," answered Rose, "but it is a funny house. What do you suppose made Lady turn in at that place? This man may not be a pirate, but there is something odd about him. This whole place is queer. I almost wish we had stayed in the chaise."

Under the two windows that faced toward the woods ran a long box-like seat, and in one corner of the room stood a shoemaker's bench, with its rows of awls, needles threaded with waxed thread, hammers, sharp knives, tiny wooden pegs, and bits of leather; a worn boot lay on the floor as if the man had started up from his work at Mr. Freeman's rap.

"What's that, Rose?" questioned Anne, pointing to a piece of iron that could be seen extending from beneath an old blanket which lay under the bench.

"It's a rifle!" answered Rose. "Look, Anne! Quick, before he comes back. I believe there are a lot of guns there."

Anne knelt down to lift the blanket. Rose was close beside her, leaning over to see what the blanket might conceal, when the kitchen door swung open and the man entered. As he looked at the two girls his face darkened again, and he came quickly forward.

"Aha!" he muttered. "It's just as I thought. Pretty clever of the old Tory to bring these girls along to peek about and find out all they can," but the girls did not hear him until he stood beside them, and then his scowl was gone and he spoke pleasantly: "A good many rifles for one man, but they are not all mine. I'm storing them for friends."

"Where's father?" asked Rose, a little anxiously.

"He's giving the pretty horse a rub down," answered the man; "now there's a better room for young ladies than this old kitchen," he continued. "Just come this way," and he opened a door into a long dark passage, into which the girls followed him.

"Right in here," said the man, opening a door at the further end of the hall, and holding it ajar for the girls to pass in.

"It's all dark!" exclaimed Anne, who had been the first to enter. Rose was close behind her and as Rose crossed the threshold the heavy door swung to behind them. They heard bolts shot and then all was quiet.

Rose sprang against the door with all her strength, but instantly realized that it was useless to try to open it. "Father! Father!" she screamed, and Anne, hardly knowing what she said, called also "Father!"

"It's dark as pitch," whispered Anne, clutching at Rose's dress; "there can't be a window in this room, or we'd see light somewhere."

The two girls clung together, not knowing what next might befall them.

"There may be some other door," said Rose after they had screamed themselves hoarse. "We must not be frightened, Anne, for father is sure to look for us. Let's go round the room and try and find a door. We can feel along the wall," so the two girls began to grope their way from the door.

"These inside walls are brick!" exclaimed Rose, as her hands left the wooden framework of the door. "Oh, Anne, I do believe it is a sort of prison all walled inside." Just then their feet struck against something hard and round which rolled before them with a little rumble of sound. Rose leaned down. "They're cannon-balls," she whispered. "Oh, Anne! There's a whole pile of them. Don't go another step; we'll fall over them. I do believe the man is a pirate, or else a Tory." For in those troublous times the Americans felt that a Tory was a dangerous enemy to their country.

As the girls groped about the room they came to a heavy iron chest, and sat down, realizing that all they could do was to wait until Mr. Freeman should discover them.

"Don't be afraid, Anne," said Rose, putting her arm about her little companion, and felt surprised when Anne answered in a hopeful voice:

"Rose, look! Right up on that wall there's a window. I can see little edges of light."

"So there is, but it's too high to do us any good; we can't reach it," answered Rose.

"Well, I'm glad it's there," said Anne.

Now and then they heard the far-off roar of the thunder, but at last it seemed to die away, and little edges of light showed clearly around the shuttered window on the further wall. The girls watched it, and, their eyes becoming used to the shadowy room, they could now distinguish the pile of cannon-balls in the opposite corner, and behind them a small cannon and a keg. They could see, too, the outlines of the doorway.

"How long do you think we shall have to stay here?" whispered Anne, as the dreary fearful moments dragged by.

"I don't know, dear," answered the elder girl, "but we mustn't be afraid."

The hours went by and the little edge of light around the high shuttered window began to fade a little, and the girls knew that the long summer day was fading to twilight, and that it had been about noon when they came to the house. A great fear now took possession of Rose's thoughts, the fear for her father's safety. She was sure that unless some harm had befallen him he would have found them before this time.

"Rose!" Anne's sharp whisper interrupted her thoughts. "If I could get up to that window I could get out and go after help. The window isn't so very high; it isn't as if we were up-stairs."

At that very moment the big door swung open, and the man entered. He had a candle in one hand and carried an armful of rough gray blankets which he dropped on the floor beside the girls, and instantly, without a word, departed, and the girls heard the bolts shot on the outside.

"Those blankets are for us to sleep on. Oh, Anne, what has he done to my dear father?" and Rose began to cry bitterly.

"Rose, he's coming back!" warned Anne, but the girl could no longer restrain her sobs and their jailer entered, this time carrying the big lunch basket which Aunt Hetty had put under the seat when they drove off so happily from Brewster.

"Here's your own grub," said the man roughly. "Your father'll have to put up with what I give him."

"You—you—won't kill my father, will you?" sobbed Rose.

"Oh, no, no!" answered the man, and then apparently regretting his more friendly tone added, "But I reckon I ought to, coming here a-peekin' an' a-pryin' into what don't concern him," and he set the basket down on the iron chest with such a thud that it fairly bounced.

"Oh, he wasn't; I was the one who peeked at the guns," said Anne.

"Oho! Peekin' at the guns! Well, I've got you now where you can't peek much," came the gruff answer.

"Won't you leave the candle?" asked Rose.

"I guess not," he answered with a little laugh, and pointed toward the keg. "Look at that keg! Well, it's full of powder, and powder's too sca'se an article these days to leave a candle in the same room with it."

"But we can't see to eat," pleaded Anne. "We'll be real careful; we won't go near the corner."

For a moment the man hesitated; then he set the candle down on the chest beside the basket.

"All right," he said. "I'll leave it; 'twon't burn more than an hour." He looked down at Rose's tear- stained face, and added, "Ain't no cause to cry about your father; he's had a good supper, and I ain't goin' to hurt him."

"Oh, thank you!" and Rose looked up at him gratefully.

The door had hardly swung to before Anne whispered, "Rose, Rose, I must get out of that window some way. You know I must. It's too small for you, but I'm sure I could get through."

"Let's eat something before you think about that," suggested Rose, who began to feel more hopeful now that she knew her father was safe, and opened the big basket. The man had brought them a pitcher of cool water, and the girls ate and drank heartily.

"Aunt Hetty would be surprised if she knew where we were eating these lovely doughnuts," said Anne, holding up the delicately browned twisted cruller.

"Anne, if we could push this chest under the window I could stand on it and try to open the window and if I can open it, then I will lift you up and you can crawl through," said Rose, biting into a chicken sandwich.

Anne nodded, watching the candle with anxious eyes, remembering that their jailer had said that it would burn but an hour.

"Now, Anne," said Rose, after they had satisfied their hunger, and closed the basket, "we must try to push the chest."

To their surprise it moved very easily, and they soon had it directly under the window. Rose was on top of it in an instant, and Anne held the candle as high as she could reach so that Rose could examine the fastening.

"Why, Anne, it pushes right out," said Rose. "It's only hooked down. Look!" and she pushed the heavy square outward. "But it doesn't go very far out," she added. "I wonder if you can crawl through. I do believe this shutter is shingled on the outside, so that nobody could tell there was a window. Oh, Anne! Isn't this a dreadful place!" Rose peered cautiously out of the open space. "Blow out the candle," she said quickly, drawing back into the room. "He might be outside and see the light." Anne instantly obeyed.

"Now, Anne, dear," said Rose, "if you can get out what are you going to do?"

"I'll run back to the road as fast as I can go and get some people to come back here and rescue you," said Anne.

"Yes, but you had best go on; you know there are no houses for a long way on the road we came, and we must be nearer the Suet settlement than any other. You won't be afraid, Anne!"

"No, Rose," declared the little girl, "and if I think of you shut up here, even if I am afraid, I shall keep on until I find somebody and bring him to help you."

"That's splendid, Anne!" answered Rose. "Now step here beside me, and I'll lift you up."

CHAPTER VIII

THROUGH THE WINDOW

"HOLD tight, Anne," whispered Rose.

Anne had succeeded in squeezing through the narrow window space, and Rose, leaning out as far as possible, kept a firm grasp on the little girl's hands.

"I'm going to let go now," whispered Rose; "try to drop easily, Anne," and in an instant Anne's feet touched the soft earth.

Rose watched her jump up and a moment later vanish in the thick growth of trees. Then she hooked the window securely, and sat down again on the iron chest. Her arms and shoulders felt lame and sore from holding Anne, but after a moment she forgot the ache and her thoughts turned to her father, and to brave little Anne traveling off through the darkness of the summer's night to bring help to her friends.

The house was so closely surrounded by woods that Anne had to move very carefully. The storm was over, but it was very dark in the shadow of the trees. For a few moments she wandered about, not quite knowing if she were moving in the right direction, but at last she found herself in the rough path up which Lady had made her way from the main road. Once or twice she stumbled and nearly fell over stumps of trees, but at last she reached the junction, and now the moonlight enabled her to see the white line of the sandy road stretching far ahead.

"I can run now," she whispered to herself, and sped away, her moccasin-covered feet making no sound as she ran. All at once Anne stopped suddenly, for coming down the road toward her were a number of dark figures. They were so near that she could hear the sound of their voices. Anne turned quickly to the roadside and crouched behind a bunch of low-growing shrubs. As the men came nearer one of them said:

"'Twas about here I saw something run into the woods."

"A fox, maybe," answered one of his companions.

"Maybe, and maybe not. It's not the time to take chances of a spy being about with those guns stored at Bill Mains'. I'm going to have a look around here and make sure," and the man turned straight toward the place where Anne crouched, fairly trembling with fear, for she had heard the man speak of the guns, and was quite sure that these men were Tories, as she supposed Bill Mains to be. She moved unconsciously, and the rustling betrayed her whereabouts, and the man took hold of her shoulder and drew her out into the road.

"Look at this! A little girl! Where's your father?" he demanded, drawing Anne toward his three companions, who were evidently too surprised to speak.

"Where's your father?" he repeated, giving Anne a little shake.

"He—he's at sea," half sobbed Anne, hardly daring to lift her head, and wondering what dreadful fate would befall her if these men should discover that she had just escaped from Bill Mains' house, and that she knew all about the guns hidden there.

"Don't be rough with the little maid, Dan," said one of the men; "it's early in the evening yet, and no harm in a child being on the road. Like as not she hid there from fear of us. Do you live near here, little one?"

Anne now ventured to look up, but in the dusk could only see that the man who spoke so kindly was bareheaded, while the others wore slouch hats which shaded their faces.

"No, sir," she answered.

"There's no house for miles," declared the man who had discovered Anne, "and there's some older person about, you may be sure."

As he spoke Anne said to herself that she would not let them know how she came there. "If I do perhaps they will kill Mr. Freeman," thought the frightened child. So when they questioned her she would not answer, and the men now had some reason to believe that Anne had older companions who might indeed be spies upon those who sympathized with the Americans.

"Is it safe to go to Mains' house?" questioned one of the men, and there was a little talk among them over the matter, but they decided to go on; and, holding Anne fast by the hand, the man who had drawn her out from her hiding-place led the way, and Anne had not been away from the shingled house but an hour or two before she found herself again at the front door.

In response to a low whistle the door opened and the men filed into the room. Bill Mains, holding a candle in his hand, stood in the little passageway and as he saw Anne he nearly let the candle fall, and exclaimed in amazement:

"Where did you find that child? I had her double locked up in the brick room."

"Are you sure of it?" asked the man who kept so tight a grasp on Anne's arm that the mark of his fingers showed for several days after.

"Of course I'm sure; locked two of them up there before the thunder-storm, and have their father tied up in the kitchen. Tory spies they are."

At the sound of the hated words Anne exclaimed: "Indeed we are not Tory spies. We are not either of those things. Mr. Freeman is a patriot, and his son is with Washington. How dare you say we are Tories and treat us so!" and the little girl quite forgot her fear, and, as the hold on her arm loosened, she took a step away from the man and said: "We were going to Boston, and going to stop at Suet to see Captain Sears, and that man," and she pointed at Bill Mains, "shut us up because Rose and I peeked under a blanket at some guns."

As Anne stopped speaking the men looked at one another in surprise. At last the bareheaded man began to laugh, and the others joined in; all but Bill Mains, who looked somewhat ashamed.

"You've been a bit too cautious, I reckon, Bill," said the man who had found Anne. "Mr. Freeman of Boston is known as a loyal man. Did he not tell you who he was?"

"I gave him no chance after I found this little maid looking at the guns I had covered with blankets," confessed Mains. "I told him I'd gag him if he said one word, and I reckon he thought he had fallen into the hands of a rank Tory. Who are you, little maid?" and he turned kindly toward Anne.

"I am John Nelson's daughter, who is at sea on the 'Yankee Hero,' and I live with Uncle Enos and Aunt Martha Stoddard in Province Town, but now I am going with Rose Freeman for a visit in Boston," explained Anne, who could hardly realize that these men were now kindly disposed toward her, and that Bill Mains was sadly ashamed to have so ill treated his unexpected guests. "You must let Rose right out of that dark room," she added hastily.

"I should say so. You shall open the door yourself, little maid," answered Mains. "You boys go on to the kitchen and get Mr. Freeman's pardon for me if you can," and he turned and led Anne toward the room where Rose was locked in.

When Rose saw Anne standing in the doorway she exclaimed: "Oh, Anne, has he brought you back!" in such an unhappy voice that Bill Mains felt very uncomfortable.

"It's all right, Rose. You are to come right out where your father is. There are some nice men out there," declared Anne, clasping her hands about Rose's arm.

"Oh! then you found help," and there was a world of relief in Rose's voice as Anne led her out of the room, which Mr. Mains did not forget to lock carefully behind them.

"He thought we were Tory spies; that's why he locked us up," Anne explained, in a tone that almost seemed to praise Mr. Mains for such precaution.

"Tory spies, indeed!" said Rose, sending a scornful glance in his direction. "He should have known better. Where is my father?"

"Right this way, miss," replied Mr. Mains humbly, and the girls followed him to the kitchen where they found Mr. Freeman surrounded by the four men who had brought Anne back to the house.

Rose's father was as ready to pardon the mistake as Bill Mains was eager to have him.

"It's worth a little trouble to find we have such good men ready to defend our cause," he declared, "but I am afraid my girls here are pretty tired, and if you can give them a room without cannon and powder, I'm sure they will sleep well," as indeed they did in a neat little chamber into which Mr. Mains conducted them, bringing in the little trunk which had been strapped on the back of the chaise.

Mr. Freeman had believed that he was in the hands of the Tories, so that he did not greatly blame his host for being doubtful regarding him.

"It will delay us a little on our journey, but it is no great matter," he said pleasantly in response to Mains' repeated apologies. Then Mains explained that this house had been built of brick, and then boarded over and covered with shingles, as a storehouse for supplies for the American army. The four men had just returned from carrying powder to a couple of Yankee boats at Plymouth. These boats were among the many privateers that cruised about during the Revolution, harassing English vessels, and often capturing rich prizes, and helping the American cause. They stayed late in the evening talking with Mr. Freeman, and listening with interest to what he could tell them of affairs in Boston; and when they started off on their way toward Brewster they promised to let his brother know of the mistake, which seemed to them a very good joke on their friend Mains.

Mr. Mains was up at an early hour the next morning, and Mr. Freeman declared the breakfast to be the best that he had ever tasted. There was broiled partridge, hot corn bread, a big dish of freshly picked blueberries, and plenty of good milk; and Anne and Rose thought that nothing could be better, and even decided that Mr.

Mains did not look like a pirate after all. "For I don't believe pirates wear brown gingham aprons, do you, Rose?" said Anne, watching Mr. Mains awkwardly tying his apron strings.

Lady had been well cared for, and was rested and ready for the journey when Mr. Mains led her up to the door for the girls to enter the chaise.

"I'm mighty sorry," he repeated as he helped the girls in, "sorry, I mean, to have locked you folks up; but real glad to know you," and he waved them a smiling good-bye, as Mr. Freeman carefully guided Lady along the rough way to the main road.

"Well, Anne, I guess you'll remember this journey all your life," said Rose, as they reached the highway and Lady trotted briskly along as if glad to find her feet on good sand again. "Just think, father," she continued, "of all that has happened to her since she left Province Town, and she's not in Boston yet."

"Things happened when I went to Boston before," said Anne, remembering her brief visit to Newbury-port, when she had safely carried a paper of importance to loyal Americans.

"I think all will go smoothly now," said Mr. Freeman, "but it was a very brave thing for a little girl to start off alone for help, as you did last night, Anne," and he looked kindly down at the little girl beside him. "Had we indeed been held prisoners by Tories you might have secured help for us, as you thought to do."

"But she really did help us, father," said Rose; "it was Anne who made them understand who we really were. I do believe we might be shut up still if Anne had not found a way to help us. Your father will be proud of you, Anne, when I tell him the story."

It made Anne very happy to have Mr. Freeman and Rose praise her, and she quite forgave the man who had pulled her from behind the bushes, and whose finger marks she could still feel on her arm.

"I hope it won't rain to-day," said Mr. Freeman. "We ought to get to Sandwich by noon, and after Lady has rested, we'll go on as far as we can. Lady seems as anxious to get to Boston as we do," for the big horse was traveling at a rapid pace, and going as if she enjoyed it.

"You shall go and see Faneuil Hall when you are in Boston, Anne," promised Rose, "and Mr. Hancock's fine house. It has terraces and stone steps, and the English officers would well like to take up their quarters there."

"They seem well satisfied with Vardy for a landlord at the 'Royal Exchange,'" answered Mr. Freeman smilingly. "Look, there is a wasp's nest as big as a bucket," and Mr. Freeman pointed his whip toward a huge gray ball hanging from the branch of a partly decayed tree near the road.

"It's a beauty," said Rose, leaning out to see the wonderful ball of gray paper which swung from the branch above them.

Mr. Freeman turned Lady to the further side of the road and said, "If the wasps have deserted their house, as they sometimes do at this season, I'd like to get it to take home to the children. I never saw so large a nest. I can soon find out," he concluded.

The brown horse stood quietly while Mr. Freeman and the girls got out of the chaise.

"Stay here a moment," said Mr. Freeman, and he walked back toward the tree and threw a small round stone at the nest. It hit the mark, but no angry wasps appeared. Another stone touched it more forcibly, and, when the third failed to bring a single wasp from the nest, Mr. Freeman declared that he knew it was vacant, and cutting a branch from a slender birch tree with his pocket-knife, which he speedily made into a smooth pole, he managed to secure the nest without damaging it and brought it proudly back to show to Rose and Anne, neither of whom had ever seen one before.

"It's just like paper," said Anne admiringly, touching it carefully.

"That's just what it is," said Mr. Freeman. "I expect men learned from wasps how to make paper. For wasps go to work in a very business-like way. They chew up dead and crumbling wood and spread it out smoothly, and when it dries and hardens there is a sheet of paper, all ready to be used as one of the layers for this dry warm nest. Men make paper by grinding up wood or linen rags."

"You can put the nest in our lunch-basket, father," said Rose. "Frederick and Millicent will think it the most wonderful thing they have ever seen."

Frederick and Millicent were Rose's younger brother and sister. Frederick was about Anne's age, but little Millicent was only six years old.

Lady turned her head as if to ask why they were lingering so far from a good stable; and Rose and Anne stopped a moment before getting in the chaise to rub her soft nose and tell her that she would soon be in Sandwich and should have a good feed of oats for her dinner.

CHAPTER IX

LADY DISAPPEARS

"WE shall reach the tavern in good season for dinner," said Mr. Freeman, as they drove into the village of Sandwich.

It seemed a very wonderful thing to the little maid from Province Town to drive up to the inn, with its big painted sign swinging from a post near the road, and she took hold of Rose's hand as if half afraid.

Rose looked down at her little friend with a smiling face.

"Why, Anne," she said laughingly, "you were not a bit afraid to start off through the woods alone, or to journey with Indians, and here you are trembling because you are going into this little tavern for dinner."

Anne managed to smile, but she kept a tight clasp on Rose's hand. It was not that she was frightened, but as she stepped from the chaise she had heard one of the loiterers about the door exclaim, "Look at the child, bareheaded and wearing moccasins," and her quick glance had comprehended the exchange of smiles; and Anne now felt uncomfortable and realized that she was not suitably dressed to travel in the high chaise. She looked at Rose, with her pretty dress of blue dimity, and white hat with its broad ribbon, her neat shoes and stockings, and realized that there was a great contrast in their appearance. Anne was very silent all through the meal and ate but little. Even Mr. Freeman began to notice that she was very silent and grave, and thought to himself that the little girl might be homesick.

"We can drive to Plymouth this afternoon," he said, as they finished their dinner. "It is only about twenty miles, and we can get there early in the evening."

Anne knew all about Plymouth. From the hill in Province Town she had looked across the water to Plymouth, and Uncle Enos had told her that many years ago a band of Pilgrims from England had landed at Province Town, and then sailed on and settled in Plymouth. Uncle Enos had wondered at it, and had shook his head over a people who would willingly settle in any other place than Province Town.

The road now followed the shore very closely, and Rose was interested in watching the boats, and the many flocks of wild sea-birds circling about in the summer air. But Anne leaned back in the corner of the chaise silent and troubled. The more she thought about her lack of all the things that Rose had the more unhappy she became. "They will all be ashamed of me when I get to Boston," she thought," and I have no money to buy things, and it will be three weeks or more before my dear father will reach Boston. Oh, dear!" And Anne, for the moment, wished herself back on the Province Town sands where a bareheaded, moccasin-shod little girl could be as happy as the day was long.

The sun had set, and it was in the cool of the early evening when they drove through Plymouth's main street. They were all tired and quite ready for bed. It seemed a very large town to Anne, with its meeting-houses and stores, but she was glad that it was nearly dark and hoped that no one would notice that she had no hat or sunbonnet.

"If I had not run away Aunt Martha would have seen to it that I had things like other girls," and she said to herself that "always, always, after this I'll tell Aunt Martha before I do things."

"To-morrow night we'll be in Boston, Anne! Think of that," said Rose happily, when the landlady had shown them to the comfortable chamber that they were to occupy for the night. "Father says we'll start by sunrise, and give Lady a rest at Scituate. Just think of all I shall have to tell when I get home. And then we'll go to the shops the very next day. Oh, Anne! I can't keep the secret another minute," and Rose came to the window where Anne stood looking out, and putting her arm over the younger girl's shoulder whispered in her ear: "Captain Stoddard gave me two golden guineas to spend for you, Anne. He said your father left them to buy clothes for you. I planned not to tell you until we were really in the shops and ready to purchase, but I thought it too good news to keep longer," and Rose smiled down at her little friend.

"Two guineas to buy clothes!" Anne's voice sounded as if such good fortune was almost beyond belief.

"And I can have a hat, and shoes and stockings, since my own were left behind in the wigwam?" she said questioningly.

"Indeed you can. And mother will go with us, and I doubt not you will have a pretty dress and slippers as well as shoes, and many fine things, for two guineas is a large sum to spend."

"Perhaps I shall not need to spend it all for clothes," said Anne; "then I can buy a present for Aunt Martha and Uncle Enos, and perhaps something for Amanda."

"Amanda!" echoed Rose. "Well, Anne, I would not take her home a gift; she does not deserve one from you."

Anne was silent, but she was excusing Amanda in her thoughts. As Amos so often said of Jimmie Starkweather that "nothing ever happens to Jimmie," so did Anne think of Amanda. She somehow felt sorry for Amanda, and had quite forgiven the ugly slaps her playmate had given her.

It took Anne a good while to go to sleep that night. Blue dimity dresses and shining slippers danced before her wakeful eyes, and a white ribbon to tie back her hair. Already she was trying to decide what her present to Amanda should be; and it seemed to her that she had just gone to sleep when Rose was shaking her gently and saying: "Time to get up."

The travelers were all in the best of spirits that morning: Rose, happy to be so near home, Anne delighted at the prospect of having dresses like the girls who lived in Boston, and Mr. Freeman had had the best of news from Plymouth friends, who declared that news from Philadelphia had been received stating that the Congress there was agreed upon declaring the independence of America.

" 'Tis what Mr. Samuel Adams has worked so hard for," Mr. Freeman told the girls; "and when the Congress has fully determined upon the form of the declaration word will be sent post-haste to Boston; and I trust, too, that Mr. Adams may be spared for a visit to his family. He has been absent from Boston for a year past."

Mr. Freeman had asked the landlord to furnish them with a luncheon, as he did not know if there would be a suitable place to procure food in Scituate; and with a bag of oats for Lady fastened on top of the little trunk, and a basket of luncheon under the seat of the chaise, the travelers could choose just when and where to stop.

"We'll keep a sharp outlook for a good clear stream of water," said Mr. Freeman.

"And I hope we can stop near the shore," said Rose; "I'd like to go in wading."

Anne thought that it would not make much difference where they stopped. The fragrant summer air, the pleasant shadow of the trees along the road, and the hope of soon being in Boston so filled her thoughts that where or what she ate seemed of little consequence.

Several hours after leaving Plymouth they found themselves on a pleasant stretch of road bordering the water.

"There is the very beach for wading!" exclaimed Rose happily, and even as she spoke they heard the splash of falling water and just before them was a rough bridge of logs over a rapid stream of clear water. Lady nearly stopped, and gave a little whinny as if asking for a drink.

"Just the place!" declared Mr. Freeman; "and here's a good piece of greensward in the shade for Lady," and he turned into a little grassy field beyond the bridge where a big beech tree stood, making a grateful circle of shade.

"Lady must have a couple of hours' rest," said Mr. Freeman, "so you girls can go down to the beach or do whatever you like until you are ready for luncheon."

The girls took off their shoes and stockings and ran down to the water's edge, and were soon wading about enjoying the cool water. After a little while they tired of wading and went up on the dry warm sand. Patches of bayberry bushes grew near the shore, and their fragrant leaves and small gray berries at once attracted Rose's attention. She had never before seen this shrub, a species of myrtle, and Anne was delighted to find something that she could tell the elder girl.

"It's bayberry, Rose. Just rub the leaves between your fingers and see how sweet it smells," she said. "Aunt Martha makes candles of these little green berries, and likes them better than tallow candles. When you snuff them out they make all the room smell just like this," and Anne held the bruised leaves up for Rose to smell.

"I don't see how candles could be made of these little berries," said Rose.

"And Aunt Martha makes a fine salve from them, too," continued Anne. "When she makes the candles I gather the berries, quarts and quarts, and she boils them in a kettle, and then skims off the top, and boils it again, and then turns it into the molds."

"Come to luncheon, girls!" called Mr. Freeman, and they ran back to the grassy field and the shade of the beech tree. On one side Lady was nibbling her oats happily. The lunch basket stood open; Mr. Freeman handed Rose a small tin drinking cup, and the girls ran down to the brook for a drink of the clear water.

"Cape Cod twists about Massachusetts Bay like a long arm, doesn't it, father?" said Rose, as they all seated themselves around the lunch basket.

Mr. Freeman laughed at Rose's description of the Cape, but nodded his head in agreement.

"I believe it does, my dear," he answered. "Province Town is the hand curved in, and Truro the wrist; Chatham must be the elbow, and now we are getting pretty well up to the shoulder."

After luncheon they all went back to the shore, and picked up many tiny shells. Some of these were clear white, and others a delicate pink. Mr. Freeman told them that the Indian women pricked tiny holes, with a small sharp-pointed awl, in these shells and strung them like beads, and Rose and Anne thought it would be a fine plan to carry a quantity of shells to Boston and string them into necklaces.

The time went swiftly, and when Mr. Freeman said that Lady had now had a good rest and would be quite ready to start on, the girls reluctantly left the beach and walked slowly toward the chaise.

"I wonder where father and Lady are?" said Rose, and as she spoke Mr. Freeman came running across the little green field.

"Lady is gone! Stolen, I'm afraid," he called out.

The girls looked at him in amazement.

"She was securely fastened, and even if she got loose would not have gone far," he continued, "and there is no trace of her." Mr. Freeman's face was very anxious, and Rose exclaimed:

"But who could take Lady, father? We have not seen a person since we left Plymouth."

"Some strolling person," answered Mr. Freeman; "perhaps some frightened Tory from one of the loyal settlements on his way toward a place of safety."

Anne stood silent, holding up the skirt of her dress filled with the pretty shells.

"And shall we have to walk to Boston?" asked Rose.

"And leave this good chaise? I think not; though I hardly know how we can remain here," said Mr. Freeman.

For an hour or more they searched the nearby woods and up and down the road, but there was no trace to be found of Lady, nor did they find anything to tell them of how she had vanished.

"Your mother told me that it was no time for a visit so far from home," said Mr. Freeman, "and if Lady is indeed stolen I shall have good reason to wish that I had stayed at home. I hardly dare send you girls along the road alone, but if I leave this chaise it may disappear as Lady has done."

"Where could we go, father?"

"We are not far from Scituate, and any of the settlers who have a horse would come back and get the chaise," he answered. "I do not know of any harm that could befall you if you keep in the highway."

"Of course we must go," Rose decided quickly, and Anne looked at her friend admiringly, thinking, as she so often did, that she would like to be exactly like Rose Freeman.

In the excitement of discovering that Lady had disappeared Rose had dropped all the pretty shells she had gathered, but Anne was holding her skirt tightly clasped.

"Put your shells in the lunch basket, Anne," said Mr. Freeman; "I'll pick up those you have dropped, Rose. We shall reach Boston some time, and you will be glad of these to remind you of an adventurous journey," and his smile made the girls ready to start off with better courage.

"Stop at the first house on the road," directed Mr. Freeman; "tell them who you are, and what has befallen us, and ask them to come to my assistance, and for permission to stay at the house until I come for you."

"Yes, father," replied Rose, and then she and Anne started down the road. They kept in the shade for some distance, then the road ran up a long sandy hill where the sun came down fully upon them, and before they reached the summit they were very warm and tired.

"There's a house!" exclaimed Anne, as they stopped to rest on the top of the hill.

"Thank goodness!" exclaimed Rose. "And it's a farmhouse. See the big barns. There are sure to be horses there."

The girls quite forgot the heat, and ran down the sandy hill and hurried along the road, which now was a smoother and better one than any over which they had traveled, and in a short time were near the comfortable farmhouse. A woman was standing in the doorway watching them.

"Where in the world did you girls come from," she called out as they opened the gate, "in all this heat? Come right in. I should think your folks must be crazy to let you walk in the sun. Was that your father who went galloping by on a brown horse just now?"

As soon as the woman finished speaking Rose told her their story.

"Then that man had stolen your horse! A Tory, I'll wager; and like enough a spy," said the woman; "and my menfolks all away. There are two horses in the pasture; if you girls can catch one of 'em and ride it back to where your father's waiting, why, you're welcome."

Anne and Rose looked at each other almost in dismay. Neither of them had ever been on the back of a horse, and to go into a pasture and catch a strange horse seemed to them very much like facing a wild beast.

"We'll try," said Rose with a little smile.

"I thought you would," said the woman approvingly. "I'd go myself, but I've got bread in the oven, and I must see to it."

The woman led the way to a shed and filling a shallow pan with oats from a big bin, handed it to Rose, saying: "You go right through those bars—leave 'em down; I'll put 'em up for you—and shake these oats and call 'Range, Range,' and the old horse will be sure to come, and the colt will follow."

Rose took the pan, and Anne pulled back the heavy bars, and they went a few steps beyond the fence into the pasture and began to call "Range! Range!"

In a moment there was the thud, thud of hoofs and two black horses came dashing down the pasture. Their long manes and tails gave them a terrifying look to the two girls, who, nevertheless, stood their ground, Rose holding out the pan as the woman had bidden her.

"Oh, Rose! They'll run right over us!" exclaimed Anne, watching the horses rushing toward them so swiftly.

CHAPTER X

AUNT ANNE-ROSE

BUT the horses came to a sudden stop a few feet from where the girls stood. Then one turned and rushed away, kicking up his heels as if to say: "I'm not to be caught!"

Rose kept on calling "Range! Range!" and shaking the pan, and the other horse stepped forward and stuck his nose into the dish.

"Grab hold of his mane, Anne. Quick! and hold on tight!" said Rose; "the woman is coming now with the bridle."

Anne obeyed, holding fast to the black mane until Mrs. Pierce came running from the barn, bringing a blanket and a bridle.

"I'm glad you caught Range," she said; "he's used to a saddle, and the colt is wild as a deer." While she talked she was strapping the blanket securely on the horse's back, and now slipped the bit into his mouth.

"The little girl better go," she continued, nodding toward Anne. "You just climb that fence, and I'll lead Range alongside and you can get on his back nicely. Sit boy fashion; it's safer. No sense as I can see in a girl jest hanging on to one side of anything," and almost

109

before she knew it Anne found herself on the back of the black horse.

Mrs. Pierce, who had told the girls her name on the way to the pasture, led Range out into the road and headed him in the right direction.

"If he don't go fast enough kick your heels against his sides and call to him," directed the woman, handing the reins to Anne, and giving the horse a sharp slap that sent him off at a good pace.

It seemed to Anne as if she were going up into the air, or over the horse's head. But somehow she managed to keep on Range's back, though she did not dare to give a backward look.

"Range will bring your pa back in no time, don't you worry," said Mrs. Pierce, giving Rose a kindly pat on the shoulder; then exclaiming, "The bread!" she ran back to the house, leaving Rose looking down the road, and wondering, a little fearfully, if Anne would reach the big beech tree without being thrown into the road.

Then she looked the other way, in the direction of Boston, and wondered what would befall Lady.

"Come in, my dear, out of this hot sun," Mrs. Pierce called from the doorway, and Rose went slowly up the path and entered the big square room at the right of the small square entry.

"You sit right down and I'll bring you a drink," and Mrs. Pierce drew forward a comfortable rocking-chair

"YOU CAN GET ON HIS BACK"

for her young guest, and was soon back with a cup of milk and a square of fresh gingerbread.

"I should admire to have a girl just like you," declared Mrs. Pierce, taking the empty cup. "I can see that you've a real good disposition, and a girl would be a sight of company to me."

Then Rose told her about her own mother, and had begun to tell her Anne Nelson's little history, when Mrs. Pierce again exclaimed: "My bread!" and hurried off to the kitchen.

Rose went to the open window and looked out, wondering how long it would be before her father would reach the farmhouse, and it seemed a long time to wait in spite of the friendly kindness of Mrs. Pierce.

The black horse went along at an easy pace, and after a little Anne ceased to be afraid, held the bridle-reins more easily, and even ventured to look about a little.

"Things keep happening," she thought. "I hope nothing has carried off Mr. Freeman and the chaise!"

Mr. Freeman was standing in the roadway, and as he saw Range with Anne on his back coming rapidly toward him he gave an exclamation of surprise. At a word the horse stopped, and Mr. Freeman lifted Anne from his back.

"A man went by Mrs. Pierce's with Lady before we got there," said Anne, after she had told him of the farmhouse, of Mrs. Pierce, and of catching Range.

While she talked Mr. Freeman was harnessing Range into the chaise, and they were soon on the way to the farm.

Rose and Mrs. Pierce were at the gate to meet them.

"Oh, father! Can't you go after Lady?" asked Rose.

Mr. Freeman looked at Mrs. Pierce questioningly. "If Mrs. Pierce will lend me a horse I'll go at once," he replied; "there are a good many houses along the way now, and I might get some trace of the thief."

"You go right along. Take the colt; he's as fast as any horse hereabouts, and maybe you can overtake the fellow," replied Mrs. Pierce.

Mr. Freeman captured the colt, and, telling Rose not to worry if he did not return until night, started off, the colt going at a pace that made the girls exclaim in admiration.

"I'm real sorry you folks should be so set back in your journey, but it's real pleasant for me to have company," said Mrs. Pierce, with a smiling look at her young visitors. "It's days and weeks sometimes without my seeing any one but my husband and the boys. Now we'll sit down here and you tell me all about your journey."

"It's just like a story!" declared Mrs. Pierce, when they had finished. "And now you are going to Boston, and you will see the streets and shops, and churches." She gave a little sigh as she finished, and Anne and Rose wished that it was possible for Mrs. Pierce to go to Boston with them.

"I don't suppose you could mark out a little plan of Boston, could you?" she said to Rose. "I like to imagine things to myself when I'm here alone, and if I knew how the streets went, and where you lived, why, I could say to myself, 'To-day Rose and Anne are going up King Street toward the State House, and up Longacre Street to the Common,' and it would seem almost as if I saw you when I looked at the plan."

"Yes, I think I could," said Rose, and Mrs. Pierce brought a sheet of paper and a red crayon from a big desk in the corner and laid them on the table.

Mrs. Pierce and Anne watched Rose mark out the Common and the Mall. "The Mall is where the fine people walk in the afternoon," she said. "Mr. Hancock's mansion is right here, on Beacon Hill, where you get a fine view across the Charles River to Charlestown."

Then she marked Copp's Hill. "This is where the British had their guns when the great battle was fought at Bunker Hill," she said.

Mrs. Pierce listened eagerly. "I can 'most see it all!" she exclaimed. "Now show me where your house is," and Rose made a little square for her home.

"We are nearer the harbor than many houses are," she explained, "for my father owns a wharf, and it is convenient to be where he can see boats and vessels coming in."

The girls had been so interested, Rose in drawing and explaining, and Anne in listening, that time passed very rapidly, and when Rose finished Mrs. Pierce opened the door of a queer little cupboard beside the chimney and took out a small square box.

"My! Is that a gold box!" exclaimed Anne admiringly, for the box shone and glittered in the light.

"If it was I wouldn't keep it these days, when our poor soldiers need food and clothes," replied Mrs. Pierce; "it is brass, one my grandfather brought from France." As she spoke she lifted the cover and took out two little cases of brown leather, and handed one to Rose and the other to Anne. "Open the little clasps," she said.

The girls obeyed, and as the little cases opened they exclaimed admiringly, for each case held a pair of scissors, a silver thimble, a tiny emery ball and a needle book.

"My uncle brought me those when I was about your age," Mrs. Pierce said to Anne. "I never quite made out why he brought two until this very day, but I see now," and she smiled happily at her little visitors. "I see now, because I can give one to each of you girls!"

After the girls had thanked her, and tried on the thimbles, and declared that the cases were almost too nice to use, Mrs. Pierce left them for a few moments.

"Rose," exclaimed Anne, "wouldn't it be splendid if Mrs. Pierce would let us make believe that she was our aunt?"

"Perhaps she will; she told me that she hadn't any brothers or sisters, or anybody except her husband and two sons," said Rose. "We might ask her if she would be willing for us, when we talk about her to each other, to call her 'Aunt Anne Rose'!"

"If your father only gets Lady back we'll be real glad the man took her; shan't we, Rose?" said Anne thoughtfully.

"Because we found Aunt Anne Rose? Why, yes, I suppose we shall," replied Rose. "But isn't it funny she should have our names! You ask her, Anne, if she is willing for us to call her aunt."

"There!" exclaimed Mrs. Pierce, when Anne ran into the kitchen and asked the question, "if I wasn't wishing for that very thing. I count it as a real blessing that some one went off with your horse! I do indeed. And if Rose's father don't find Lady he can borrow our colt for the rest of the journey."

It was late in the afternoon before Mr. Freeman returned, but he did not bring Lady, nor had he any news of her.

Mr. Pierce and his sons returned home at nightfall, and made the travelers feel that they were as pleased as "Aunt Anne Rose" to have their guests remain for the night.

CHAPTER XI

IN BOSTON

MR. FREEMAN looked a little puzzled when he heard the girls calling Mrs. Pierce "Aunt Anne Rose," and when Mrs. Pierce told him that was really her name he thought, as the girls had, that it was almost like discovering a relative. Mr. Pierce had insisted that they should borrow the black colt for the remainder of their journey, and they were ready to start at an early hour the next morning.

Rose was tying the ribbons to her pretty hat, while Anne watched her a little wistfully, wishing that she had a hat—almost any kind of a hat, she thought—so that she might not look like "a little wild girl," as she had overheard some one call her at the Sandwich tavern. Just then she felt something placed gently on her head and saw two broad brown ribbons falling each side of her face.

"Oh!" she exclaimed, looking up in wonder.

Mrs. Pierce stood beside her. "There!" she exclaimed. "What kind of a milliner do you think I should make for the fine ladies in Boston?" and she lifted the hat from Anne's head, holding it up for the girls to see.

117

It was a round flat hat, plaited of straw. It had no trimming save a pretty bow and strings of brown ribbon, but Anne thought it was a beautiful hat.

"It's one I plaited last year," continued Mrs. Pierce, putting the hat back on Anne's head, and tying the brown ribbon under her chin. "I did it evenings, just to keep busy. I do wish I had a prettier ribbon for it."

"Is it for me?" asked Anne, almost afraid that it was almost too much good fortune to expect.

"Of course it is. 'Twill serve to remind you of your Aunt Anne," and the friendly woman smiled down at Anne's happy face.

"We will write you a letter, Aunt Anne Rose," said Rose, as they walked down the path to where the chaise awaited them, "and you will come and visit my mother in Boston, will you not?"

"Mr. Pierce has already promised that they will both come," said Mr. Freeman.

"And, Anne," and Mrs. Pierce patted the little hand she was holding so closely, "you tell your father that you have found another aunt, and that he must let you come and stay with me for a long long visit."

Then good-byes were said, and they were again started on their journey.

"No stops this time—except to ask for news of Lady—until I reach my own house," declared Mr. Freeman. " 'Tis a good cool morning and we ought to get home by midday."

"Perhaps we shall find Lady," suggested Rose. But Mr. Freeman shook his head.

"I'm afraid it will be a long time before we get any news of her," he said soberly. "I only hope the thief will not abuse her." The brown horse had always been petted and made much of, and neither Mr. Freeman nor Rose could bear to think of her in the hands of people who would not be kind to her.

Every now and then Anne would take off the plaited straw hat and look at it with admiring eyes. "I shall not have to buy a hat now, Rose," she said.

"But you will want a prettier one than that," responded her friend.

"A prettier hat!" Anne's tone seemed to say that she could not imagine a prettier hat, and she shook her head. "I sha'n't ever want any other hat," she declared. "I mean to keep this always because Aunt Anne Rose gave it to me."

The black colt sped along as if it was nothing but play to pull the big chaise. The girls told Mr. Freeman of all that Aunt Anne Rose had said about the big farm, and of her own loneliness when her husband and sons were away. Rose noticed that, although her father listened, his glance traveled sharply over the pastures as they went along; and that now and then he leaned out for a clearer view of some horse feeding near the road, and she realized that he was keeping an outlook for Lady.

But there was no sign of the pretty brown horse, and Mr. Freeman's inquiries at houses and in villages along the way did not give him any news of Lady. There was so much for Anne to see and think about that she hardly realized what a serious loss had befallen her good friends. But as they drove down Longacre Street, past Boston Common, and turned into the street where the Freemans' house stood, she saw that Rose and Mr. Freeman both looked very downcast.

"What will mother say?" Rose half whispered, as if to herself.

Mrs. Freeman was at the door to welcome them.

"And here is our little maid from Province Town," she said, putting her arm about Anne. "You are indeed welcome, dear child; and it is a fine time for a little girl to visit Boston."

Mr. Freeman had expected his wife to ask what had become of Lady, and was surprised that she did not. He led the colt toward the stable, which stood in a paved yard back of the house, and Frederick ran ahead to open the stable door.

"Upon my soul!" exclaimed Mr. Freeman, for there in her own comfortable stall was Lady, munching her noonday meal as if everything was just as usual.

"The man got here last night with Lady," explained Frederick; "he was in a great hurry to get a boat, and he told me—for mother was at a neighbor's—that you'd be coming on to-day. Was he taking a message to

American troops? Mother said that must be his business; that you'd lend Lady for no other reason," and the boy looked at his father questioningly.

"I hope that may have been his errand," said Mr. Freeman, "but I fear he was on other business. The Tories are more anxious than Americans for boats just now," and he told the boy how Lady had been stolen. "But who ever it was must have known me and where I live," he concluded; " 'tis not every thief who leaves the horse in its owner's stable."

"But your name is on the little brass plate on Lady's bridle," Frederick reminded him, "so 'twould be easy if the man were honest."

Mr. Freeman cautioned them not to tell any one but Rose's mother of their discovery of the shingled house in the woods where Bill Mains had the hidden stores.

"No one knows just whom to trust these days," he said, "and if such news was known to those who sympathize with the English they'd soon be after his guns and powder."

"I think we will have a sewing-bee," Mrs. Freeman said, when Rose had told her the story of Anne's flight from Province Town, and that the little girl had no clothing, but had two golden guineas to spend. "You and Anne will have to be busy with your needles for a part of each day until she has proper clothes. And early to-morrow morning we will walk up to Mistress Mason's shop on Cornhill and get her some shoes."

The little room that opened from Rose's chamber had a broad window which looked toward the harbor. There were white curtains at this window, tied back with crocheted bands of white cotton. The floor was painted a soft grayish brown, and there were strips of rag carpet spread beside the white covered bed, and in front of the mahogany bureau. There was a looking-glass hung over this bureau. By standing on tiptoe Anne could see herself in it. In one corner of the room was a wash-stand with a blue china bowl and pitcher. Near the window was a low table and a rocking-chair.

It was a very neat and pleasant room, and to Anne it seemed beautiful. That it opened directly into the big square chamber where Rose slept made her feel very much at home. She wished that Aunt Martha Stoddard could see it, and she went to the window and looked off across the blue waters of the harbor wishing that she could see Aunt Martha and tell her all the wonderful things that had befallen her.

It was decided that Anne was to have a pair of slippers with straps fastening around the instep, and a pair of shoes for every-day wear. Mrs. Freeman had a good store of white stockings which Rose had outgrown and from these a number were selected for Anne. When she was dressed ready to go to the shops with Mrs. Freeman and Rose the latter exclaimed:

"Mother, mayn't I open the parlor shutters so that Anne can see herself in the long mirror?"

"Why, yes; but be very careful to close them that the sun may not strike on the carpet," replied Mrs. Freeman, a little reluctantly; for the Freemans' parlor was a very grand room and opened only when company was asked to tea, or when some distinguished person came to call.

Rose turned the brass knob, pushed open the white-paneled door and tiptoed into the shadowy room. "Come in, Anne!" she called, and Anne followed. She had not seen this room when she had visited the Freemans with Uncle Enos two years before.

"Oh!" she exclaimed, half fearfully, as her feet sank into the soft carpet. Then she stood quite still until Rose had opened the paneled inside shutters at one of the large windows. She looked about her in wonder. Directly opposite the door was a fireplace with a high white mantel, and over the mantel was the portrait of a very old lady who seemed to be smiling straight at Anne.

"Come in," Rose repeated, with a little laugh of pleasure at Anne's evident admiration, and she led her little visitor toward the front of the room where a long mirror, from ceiling to floor, was fastened against the wall between the two windows. "Look at yourself, Anne. You can see the room afterward," she said, and Anne looked into the mirror and smiled, for she saw a little dark-eyed girl with smoothly braided hair, wearing a hat of plaited straw with a brown ribbon, and a dress of brown linen with a pretty frill at the neck. She looked down admiringly at her white stockings and new shoes, and then twisted her head in the hope of seeing the back of this neat little girl. She quite forgot the soft carpet, and the shining tables and cushioned chairs.

"I do wish Amanda could see me," she said; "she'd be real glad I had these fine things."

CHAPTER XII

A WONDERFUL DAY

ANNE held Rose's hand very tightly as they walked along. It seemed to the little girl that all the people of the town were out walking up and down the streets. Now and then there would be a clatter of hoofs over the cobblestone pavements and Anne would look up to see a man go by on horseback. And Mrs. Freeman told her to notice a fine coach drawn by two horses, that stood in front of the very shop they were about to enter.

"If I spend a guinea for clothes will it not be enough?" Anne questioned, as Mrs. Freeman asked a smiling clerk to show them blue dimity.

"Why, yes, Anne; I think we can manage very nicely with a guinea," responded Mrs. Freeman, who meant to supply Anne with many needful things from her own stores. "Do you wish to save one?"

Anne shook her head. "No," she responded, "but I want to buy a grand present for Aunt Martha and Uncle Enos, and something for Amanda Cary. I should like to take Amos and the Starkweather children something, but I fear there will not be enough money."

Mrs. Freeman smiled at Anne's thought for her playmates. "You can perhaps make something for some of your little friends. Would not the Starkweather children like a little work-bag or a hemstitched handkerchief?" she asked.

The thought of the Starkweather boys with work-bags and hemstitched handkerchiefs seemed very funny to Anne, and she gave a little laugh, saying, "But they are all boys."

"Oh, well, then we will make some fine candy just before you go home, and you and Rose can make some pretty boxes to put it in. So there's your present for the Starkweather boys. And you'll have a whole guinea to buy gifts for Mrs. Stoddard and the captain, and for Amanda. I suppose Amanda is your dearest friend, isn't she?" and Mrs. Freeman looked down into Anne's happy smiling face, quite sure that Mrs. Stoddard must be very glad that she had taken the little girl into her own home.

"Best friend, indeed!" exclaimed Rose, before Anne could answer. "Why, mother! Had it not been for that Amanda, Anne never would have run away."

"But Anne wants to take her a present," said Mrs. Freeman.

A little flush crept into Anne's brown cheeks. "I guess Amanda didn't mean to," she said.

The clerk was waiting patiently, and Mrs. Freeman now begged his pardon for so long delaying her purchases, and ordered enough dimity for Anne's dress. It was a light blue with a tiny white sprig, and Anne thought it the prettiest pattern that any one could imagine.

"I have plenty of nainsook in the house for your underwear, so we will not purchase that," said Mrs. Freeman, "but we will buy some good white cotton yarn so that I can take up some stockings for you. It will make work for you at odd times." For in those days children were taught that useful occupation brought as much pleasure as play, and every girl had "pieced a quilt" before she was ten years of age, worked a sampler, and usually knit all her own stockings and mittens.

"Can't Anne have some thread gloves like mine?" Rose asked, and Anne drew a quick breath of delight. "White thread gloves," she thought to herself, would be more than she could hope for, but Mrs. Freeman seemed to think it a very reasonable request, and told Rose to go with Anne to a shop on Queen Street and select a pair of gloves.

"I must go home now," she added, "for it is Saturday, and I have much to do. After you have purchased the gloves you girls can walk up to the Common if you wish; but be sure and be home in good season for dinner."

The girls both promised, and Mrs. Freeman left them, with a word of caution to be careful in crossing Long-acre Street, where there were always many teams, carriages and horsemen going back and forth.

"You are almost a young lady, aren't you, Rose?" Anne said admiringly, as she looked up at her friend.

"I suppose so," Rose replied laughingly. "See, my skirts come to my ankles, and Aunt Hetty said I must twist my braids around my head now. And I think it does become me better," and Rose put up her white-gloved hand to be quite sure that the braids were smoothly fastened.

The girls walked along the Mall, and a little way toward the Charles River. Rose met several girls of her own age who greeted Anne pleasantly. One of them asked Rose if she knew that a messenger had reached Boston with a copy of the Declaration of Independence. "It is to be read from the balcony of the State House on Tuesday," said Rose's friend. " 'Twill be a great day, and 'tis well you have reached Boston in time for it."

When Anne and Rose reached the Freeman house little Millicent was at the door waiting for them. She had a big doll in her arms and told Anne that its name was "Hetty," because Aunt Hetty Freeman had made it and sent it to her. Frederick had hung the wasp's nest in his own room, and declared that there was not another boy in Boston who possessed one. Several of his friends had already seen it, and Frederick was quite sure that he was a very fortunate boy to have it for his own.

On Sunday morning Anne was awakened by the sound of the bells of Christ Church, which was not far distant from the Freemans' house. She lay listening to the musical notes, and wondering if those could really be church-bells.

"They sound like far-off voices singing," she thought to herself. And when Mrs. Freeman, at breakfast time, told her that there were eight bells, and that they came all the way from Gloucester, England, in 1745, and were the first ring of bells in North America, they seemed even more wonderful to the little girl.

"William Shirley was Governor of Massachusetts at that time," said Mr. Freeman, "and when the bells reached Boston it was found that there was no money in the church treasury to raise them to the church belfry, and just then Boston had the good news that the colonial forces under General Pepperell had captured Louisburg. Well, every bell in Boston was ringing with triumph, and it did not take long to start a subscription and get money enough to put those fine bells where they could be heard. They were made by good English bell-makers, and there are none better," concluded Mr. Freeman. Anne thought to herself that she would be sure to remember about these wonderful bells so that she could tell Amanda.

On the morning of the 18th of July people began to gather in King Street and the vicinity of the State House, so that long before one o'clock, the time advertised when the Declaration of Independence was to be read, there was a crowd. Mr. and Mrs. Freeman with Millicent, Frederick, Rose and Anne had a very good place where they could see the little balcony where Colonel Crafts was to stand.

"Look, father! There are some of the British officers!" said Frederick.

The crowd near where the Freemans were standing stood courteously back to make way for several British officers in full military dress. They secured a place where they could hear well, and Mr. Freeman and several gentlemen exchanged smiles of satisfaction to see these officers present. When the clock struck one, Colonel Crafts, surrounded by a number of gentlemen, appeared on the balcony, and in a clear voice read the declaration announcing to the world that the American colonies were no longer subject to Britain.

What a chorus of shouts and huzzas filled the air! Frederick's cap went so high that it lodged on the State House balcony, but no one seemed to notice it, and Frederick could not recover his property until late that afternoon. There sounded the measured boom of cannon, and thirteen volleys of musketry. A military band played, and the people dispersed, quietly, and as if they had taken part in a great ceremony, as indeed they had.

"Now you girls will have to settle down; dresses do not make themselves," said Mrs. Freeman; "nor do stockings grow on trees. Your father's ship will be coming into harbor before you know it, Anne; and you must have your clothing in order, and Rose has agreed to help you. So to-morrow we must begin in earnest."

"I have a chance to send the black colt to Mr. Pierce to-morrow," said Mr. Freeman, "and I have bought a good side-saddle for Mrs. Pierce, that they may know we do not forget their great kindness."

"That is the very thing, father!" exclaimed Rose. "Now Aunt Anne Rose can ride to the village and see her friends whenever she wishes. She will not be so lonely."

"I thought of that," said Mr. Freeman.

"You girls must make up a little package for the colt to carry to your new aunt," suggested Mrs. Freeman.

Anne had her golden guinea and several shillings besides in a pretty knit purse that Rose had given her, and she was very happy to think that, out of her very own money, she could buy something for Aunt Anne Rose.

"I know what she'd like," said Anne. "I told her about the fine book that my Aunt Martha keeps in the chest. 'Tis called 'Pilgrim's Progress.' And Aunt Anne Rose said that if she had a book to read at times 'twould be as good as company."

"You girls shall step into Mistress Mason's and select a suitable book," said Mrs. Freeman. "You can write her name in it and put 'From Anne and Rose to Aunt Anne Rose'; no doubt 'twill please her. And this evening we will make some sweets to send her. We wish her to be very sure that we do not lack in gratitude."

Mistress Mason's shop in Cornhill seemed a very wonderful place to Anne, with its shelves filled with bright pewter, tall brass candlesticks, and large and small boxes. On a lower shelf at the back of the small room was a row of books. On a narrow counter stood boots, shoes, and slippers. Above this counter, fastened to a stout cord, were hung a number of dolls dressed in the latest fashion. Each one of these dolls had a small white card fastened to its sleeve.

When the girls entered they did not at first see any one in the shop, but in a moment Anne noticed that a very tiny old lady was standing behind the further counter.

"Why, she isn't any bigger than I am!" thought the little girl.

"Good-afternoon, Mistress Mason," said Rose; "this is my friend, little Anne Nelson, from Province Town."

"Not so very little, as I view it. Fully as large as I am myself. I should call her large; that is, large for a girl," responded the little white-haired woman, who was rather sensitive in regard to her size. "I see you wear good shoes," she continued, peering over the low counter and pointing a tiny finger toward Anne's feet. "I know my own shoes when I see 'em," and she laughed pleasantly. "My brother makes every shoe I sell; makes 'em right back here in his own shop, as Miss Rose Freeman well knows."

"Yes, indeed," answered Rose, "and Mistress Mason makes dolls, Anne—all those fine ones near the door."

"All but the ones with china heads; I make only bodies for the heads. The china heads come from France and cost me dear. But they are good bodies, as you can see, my dears; with joints where joints should be, and with feet and hands of soft kid. 'Tis some work, I do assure you, young ladies, to stitch fingers and toes as fingers and toes should be stitched," and Mistress Mason looked very serious indeed. "And as for making dolls with kid-covered heads, and then painting their faces and giving a good expression to eyes and mouths, I do feel that it's almost beyond me. I do indeed!"

The little old lady trotted briskly across the shop and unfastening several dolls from the line held them toward her visitors. "Now here is Lady Melissa Melvina," and Anne saw that on each of the white cards was written the name belonging to the doll on whose sleeve the card was pinned. "Lady Melissa Melvina is all kid," went on Mistress Mason, "head, body, feet and fingers; and every stitch she wears is of the best. She's worth twenty shillings. But—!" and Mistress Mason made an impressive pause and shook her head. "Could I get that amount? No. So, though 'tis far too little, you may have her for ten shillings six," and she smiled as if she were really bestowing a gift upon them.

"We did not come to buy a doll, Mistress Mason, although I'm sure Anne would like greatly to have so fine a doll as this; but we want to purchase a book," said Rose.

The little old woman was evidently disappointed. "A book, indeed," she responded. "I know not what is coming to people. Everybody, even the very children, are asking for books. We can hardly keep our shelf neatly filled, and I have half a mind not to keep them. Many a person who should buy a stout pair of shoes puts the money in books," and she shook her head as if not understanding such folly.

" 'Tis for a present," responded Rose, as if to excuse their purchase, "to a lady who lives in the country and is much alone."

"I see; well, maybe such folk find company in reading," said the shopkeeper. "Here is a book may please her," and she took up a thin volume and opened it. " 'Tis a book of verse, but 'tis well thought of. I see but little sense in verse myself; but, for verse, this reads well:

> " 'Great conquerors greater glory gain
>   By foes in triumph led than slain,' "

she read, and went on to a second couplet:

> " 'Ay me! What perils do environ
>   The man that meddles with cold iron.' "

And I declare here is what I've always said of poetry. 'Tis as true as I make good dolls:

> " 'Those that write in rhyme still make
>   The one verse for the other's sake.' "

"I think Aunt Anne Rose would like 'Pilgrim's Progress,' " Anne ventured, a little timidly, to suggest.

"Maybe. I have a fine copy. Not too large, and easy to read. 'Twill cost five shillings," and Mistress Mason put back the book of verse and took from the shelf a small square book that she handed to Rose.

The girls looked it over carefully. "But it is not like Aunt Martha's book," said Anne; " 'tis not so large, nor has it such fine pictures. These pictures are little and black."

"It tells the same story," Rose assured her, "and I know it would please Aunt Anne Rose. It will cost us two and six, sixty-two cents, apiece."

They decided to purchase it, and Mistress Mason wrapped it up in a neat package for them, and said that she hoped they would step in again. She followed them to the door, and Rose and Anne both bowed very politely as they wished her good-day.

CHAPTER XIII

ANNE'S BOOK

"ROSE," said Anne, as soon as they left the little shop, "I know what I shall buy for Aunt Martha; I shall buy her one of those fine pewter dishes."

"So you can! It will be sure to please her," replied Rose, looking kindly down at her little friend. "You are always thinking of giving people things, aren't you, Anne? My Grandmother Freeman, who lived in Wellfleet, used to say that it was a sign that a child would grow up prosperous and happy if it had the spirit to give instead of to take."

When the girls went up the brick walk to the Freeman house they saw Frederick and a number of small boys in the yard. Frederick was standing on a box with a paper in his hand, from which he was reading, and he and his companions were so interested that they did not notice the girls.

"He's playing that he's Colonel Crafts reading the Declaration," Rose whispered to Anne, as they opened the front door, and entered the house. "Fred has made believe everything that has happened here in Boston for the last two years."

"It's warm weather for candy-making," said Mrs. Freeman, as the family gathered at the supper table in the cool pleasant dining-room, "but Caroline is going to see her mother this evening, so you children can have the kitchen, and you will not have another opportunity for a long time to send Aunt Anne Rose any remembrance."

The children all declared that it was not too warm for candy-making, and as soon as Caroline, a young woman who helped Mrs. Freeman and Rose with the household work, gave them permission Rose, Anne, Millicent and Frederick went into the kitchen. Rose opened a deep drawer in a chest which stood in one corner of the room.

"Look, Anne," she said, and Anne peered in, exclaiming:

"Why, it's filled with little boxes!"

"Yes," said Rose, picking up one shaped like a heart; "stormy days, and sometimes in winter evenings, when I do not feel like knitting or sewing, I make boxes out of heavy paper or cardboard, and cover them with any bits of pretty paper or cloth that I can get. Frederick helps me. He can make even better ones than I can, and Millicent helps too," and she smiled down at the little sister who stood close beside Anne.

"Let's send Aunt Anne Rose the heart-shaped box," said Anne.

"And fill it with heart-shaped taffy," added Frederick, running toward a shelf filled with pans and kettles of various shapes and sizes, and taking down a box. "See, we have little shapes for candy," and he opened the box and took out some tiny heart-shaped pans, and dishes shaped in rounds and stars and crescents.

"My!" exclaimed Anne, "and can you make the candies in these?"

"No!" and Frederick's voice was a little scornful. "We have to boil it in a kettle, of course; then we grease the inside of these little pans with butter and turn the candy into them, and when it cools we tip them out, and there they are. Fine as any you can buy, aren't they, Rose?"

"Yes, indeed, and Frederick knows just how to take them out without breaking the candy. He is more careful than I am," said Rose, who lost no opportunity of praising her little brother and sister, and who never seemed to see any fault in them.

"Molasses taffy is the best," declared Frederick, "but you can make some sugared raisins, can't you, Rose?"

"We'll have to be very careful in putting the candy in the boxes so that it will not melt," said Rose.

Before it was time to pack the candy Mrs. Freeman came into the kitchen and untied a bundle to show the children what it contained.

"It's lovely, mother!" exclaimed Rose, lifting up a little fleecy shoulder cape of lavender wool. "Why, it's the one you knit for yourself!" and she looked at her mother questioningly.

"It seemed all I had that was pretty enough to send Mrs. Pierce," replied Mrs. Freeman.

"But she lives way off in that lonesome place where she never sees pretty things. She'd be pleased with anything," said Rose, who almost wished that her mother would keep the pretty shawl.

"That's why I want to send this to her," responded Mrs. Freeman. "If she had all sorts of nice things I wouldn't do it; I'd just send her a cake with my love."

"Send the cake, too," said Mr. Freeman, who had followed his wife. "Send the cake with my love."

"Why, so I will," said Mrs. Freeman. "Caroline made two excellent loaves of spice cake this very day and we can well spare one of them. But you children must trot off to bed. It's been a very exciting day."

Little Millicent was quite ready for bed, but neither Anne nor Rose was sleepy, and Rose followed her little friend into her room.

"See how clear the night is, Anne," she said, looking out of the window toward the harbor. "The water looks like a mirror."

Anne came and stood beside her. Her thoughts traveled across the smooth waters to the little house in Province Town. "I shouldn't wonder if Aunt Martha were looking out at the water and thinking about me," she said, drawing a little nearer to the tall girl beside her. "I wish she knew how good everybody is to me."

Rose put her arm about the little girl. "She expects everybody to be good to you, Anne," she responded; "but I have thought of something that you can do for Mrs. Stoddard that I am sure will please her, and will be something that she will always like to keep."

"What is it, Rose?" and Anne's voice was very eager.

"Let's sit down here on the window-seat, and I'll tell you. You have learned to write, haven't you, Anne?"

"Not very well," confessed the little girl.

"All the better, for what I want you to do will teach you to write as neatly as possible. I want you to write a book."

"A book!" Anne's voice expressed so much surprise and even terror that Rose laughed aloud, but answered:

"Why, yes, and you must call it 'Anne Nelson's Book,' and you must begin it by telling what Amanda Cary did to you, and how you believed that Mrs. Stoddard would be glad if you went away. And then you can write all your journey, about the Indians, the house in the woods, Aunt Anne Rose, and all that you see and do in Boston."

"I haven't any paper," said Anne, as if that settled the question.

"I have a fine blank book, every page ruled, that will be just the thing," responded Rose, "and I will help you write it. I can draw a little, and I have a box of watercolors. I will make little pictures here and there so that Mrs. Stoddard can see the places."

"Oh, Rose! That will be fine. Shall we begin the book to-morrow?"

Anne was soon in bed, but there were so many wonderful things to think of that she lay long awake.

The Freeman household rose at an early hour. After breakfast Mrs. Freeman said: "Now, Anne, we will make believe that you are my own little girl, and I will tell you what to do to help me, just as I do Rose. You see," she added with a little laugh, "that I am like Frederick. I like to play that all sorts of pleasant things are really true."

Anne smiled back. "I like to make-believe, too," she said.

"Then we'll begin right now. You can help Rose put the chambers in order, and dust the dining-room. After that Rose can show you the attic, if you want to see where the children play on stormy days, or you may do whatever you please."

"The attic will be the very place for Anne to write her book," said Rose, and told her mother of their plan.

It was a very happy morning for Anne. Rose tied a big white apron around her neck, gave her a duster of soft cloth, and showed her just how to make a bed neatly, and put a room in order. Then, when the work was finished, the girls went up the narrow stairs to the attic, a long unfinished room running the whole length of the house with windows at each end. Under one of these windows stood a broad low table. Rose had brought up the blank book, a number of pens, made from goose-quills, and a bottle of ink. She put them on the table and drew up a high-backed wooden chair for Anne. "I'll sit in this rocking-chair at the end of the table with my knitting," said Rose.

Anne looked about the attic, and thought that the Freeman children had everything in the world. There was a big wooden rocking-horse, purchased for Frederick, but now belonging to Millicent. There were boxes of blocks, a row of dolls beside a trunk, a company of tin soldiers, and on a tiny table was spread out a little china tea-set. It was rather hard for Anne to turn away from all these treasures and sit down at the table. She had never seen so many toys in all her life, and she thought she would like to bring her own wooden doll, "Martha Stoddard," that her father had made for her years ago, up to the attic to visit with these beautiful dolls of china, wax, and kid. But Rose had opened the book and stood beside the table waiting for Anne to sit down.

"How shall I begin?" questioned the little girl anxiously.

"Why, I'd begin just as if I were writing a letter," said Rose.

So Anne dipped the quill in the ink, and, with her head on one side, and her lips set very firmly together, carefully wrote: "My dear Aunt Martha."

Rose looked over her shoulder. "That is written very neatly, Anne," she said.

"Don't you want to make a picture now, Rose?" said the little girl hopefully.

Rose laughed at Anne's pleading look, but drew the book toward her end of the table, and taking a pencil from her box of drawing materials made a little sketch, directly under Anne's written words, of a little girl at a table writing, and pushed the book back toward Anne.

"Now I will knit while you write," she said.

So Anne again dipped the quill into the ink, and wrote: "This is a picture of me beginning to write a book. Rose made it." The attic was very quiet, the sound of Anne's pen, and of Rose's knitting-needles could be heard, and for a little time there was no other sound; then came a clatter of stout shoes on the stairway, and little Millicent appeared.

"See, I found this in Anne's room!" she exclaimed.

Anne looked around, and saw Millicent holding up her beloved "Martha Stoddard." With a quick exclamation she sprang up and ran toward her. "That's my doll," she exclaimed, and would have taken it, but Millicent held it tightly exclaiming:

"I want it!"

Anne stood looking at the child not knowing what to do. This doll was the dearest of her possessions. She had given her beautiful coral beads to the Indian girl, and now Millicent had taken possession of her doll. She tried to remember that she was a big girl now, ten years old, and that dolls were for babies like six-year-old Millicent. But "Martha Stoddard" was something more than a plaything to Anne; she could not part with it. But how could she take it away from the little girl?

"I want it," repeated Millicent, looking up at Anne with a pretty smile, as if quite sure that Anne would be glad to give it to her. Anne put her hands over her face and began to cry.

CHAPTER XIV

ANNE AND MILLICENT

ANNE had sprung up from her seat so quickly that she did not think of her book, pen, or ink. Her arm had given the book a careless push, sending it against and overturning the ink-bottle, and she had dropped the pen on the white paper, where it made a long ugly blot.

Rose had been quick to seize the bottle before it rolled to the floor, and was now using a big dusting cloth to wipe up the ink. Her attention was so taken with this that she did not really know what was happening, when the sound of Millicent crying made her look quickly around.

"What is the matter?" she asked, turning toward the little girls.

Anne, with her hands over her face, was evidently crying; and Millicent, grasping the wooden doll with both hands, was making as much noise as she possibly could in a series of half-angry little sobs.

"Millicent, stop this minute," said Rose, going toward them, "and you, too, Anne, and tell me what you are crying about," and, quite forgetting the inky cloth in her hand, Rose took hold of Anne's arm.

145

Anne looked up, the tears streaming down her cheeks.

"There, there," said Rose, wiping Anne's face, and leaving it almost blacker than the cloth. "Oh, what have I done!" exclaimed Rose, while Millicent's sobs ceased for a moment to be followed by a shriek of terror to see Anne's face turn black so suddenly. "Stop, Millicent," said Rose. "Come down-stairs, Anne, and I'll wash the ink off. And tell me what the matter is."

"Rose! Rose!" called Mrs. Freeman from the floor below. "What is the matter?"

"I've got ink on Anne's face and Millicent is frightened," Rose called back, drawing Anne toward the stairs. Millicent stopped crying, and finding that no one took the wooden doll from her, trotted across the attic and introduced the newcomer as "Lady Washington" to the other dolls, sat down on the floor beside them and began to play happily.

Anne followed Rose down the stairs and into the sink-room, where Rose began to scour her face vigorously.

"I don't mean to hurt you, Anne," she said laughingly, "and I'm awfully sorry I wiped your face with that dreadful inky cloth, but I have to rub hard to get it off."

"It's my—fault," Anne managed to say. "I was crying."

"There isn't any blame in crying, if you have anything to cry about," said Rose.

"Millicent wanted my doll," said Anne.

Rose did not speak for a moment. She was very fond of Anne Nelson, and thought her a very generous and thoughtful child, and could not understand why she should cry because little Millicent had taken what Rose called to herself "an old wooden doll."

"Well," she said, "Millicent won't hurt your doll."

"But she wants to keep it," said Anne, as Rose gave her face a vigorous wiping with a rough towel.

Rose made no answer. She thought it rather selfish of Anne, when they had all done so much for her, that she should be unwilling for Millicent to keep the doll.

Anne was not a dull child, and Rose's silence made her realize that she had acted selfishly; still, she could not feel that wanting to keep "Martha Stoddard" was wrong.

"There! You are quite rid of ink now," said Rose, "and there is an hour before dinner. Do you want to write some more in your book?"

"No," said Anne. It seemed to her that she should never want to write in the book again. She wished that she and "Martha Stoddard" were safe back with Aunt Martha in Province Town.

"Well, I have some errands to do for mother, so I'll run along," said Rose pleasantly, and left Anne alone in the little square room called the "sink-room," because of two sinks near the one window which over-looked the green yard at the back of the house. There was a door opening into the yard, and Anne looked out feeling more unhappy than she had since the night when Aunt Martha had sent her up-stairs.

HE HANDED HER A BALL

Frederick was in the yard. He was setting what looked to Anne like wooden bottles in a straight row at the further end of the square of greensward. Then he ran across to the open door where Anne was standing.

"Want to play bowls?" he asked.

"I don't know how," replied Anne.

"I'll show you; it's easy," replied the boy, picking up a big wooden ball and balancing it on one hand. "Come on out and try," he urged, and Anne stepped out into the yard. "Watch me! "said Frederick.

He stepped back a little, sent a keen glance toward the wooden "bottles," as if measuring the distance, then holding the ball in one hand and leaning a little sideways, swung it back and forth for a few times and then sent it rolling across the grass. It struck one of the "bottles," and that in falling sent over two more.

"Oh, I can do that!" exclaimed Anne.

"All right, try. I'll set up the pins for you," said Frederick.

Anne thought to herself that it was funny to call those wooden objects "pins."

"You'd better take a smaller ball," said Frederick, selecting one from a number lying near the door; and he handed her a ball that Anne thought was about the size of a pint dipper.

Frederick told her how to hold it, how to stand, and how to get the right motion to send it in a straight line.

"It's all in your eye, looking straight, and getting the right swing," he said.

Anne's first ball did not go half the proper distance, but she kept on trying, and before dinner time could send a ball nearly as well as Frederick himself.

"It's fun," she declared. Her face was flushed with the exercise, and her eyes shining with pleasure. For the moment she had forgotten all about the wooden doll. She and Frederick stopped in the sink-room to wash their hands before going in to dinner.

"Anne plays a good game of bowls," said Frederick, as they took their places at the table.

"I want to bowl," exclaimed little Millicent.

"You can, any time you want to," said Frederick, with his pleasant smile. "I'll show you after dinner when Rose and Anne are sewing."

Anne thought to herself that the family all wanted Millicent to do everything she wanted to, and she remembered "Martha," and wondered what Millicent had done with her beloved doll, but did not dare ask. They were all pleasant and kind to Anne, but she felt as if Rose did not look at her quite as kindly as usual.

"I have your blue dimity all basted, my dear," Mrs. Freeman said to Anne as they left the dining-room, "and you can sit with me and stitch up the seams this afternoon. Rose is to help Caroline with some cooking."

Anne felt rather glad of this, for she dreaded having Rose say something about the happening of the morning. Mrs. Freeman led the way to her pleasant chamber. A little rush-bottomed rocking-chair stood near one of the windows.

"You may sit in the little chair, Anne; that is where Rose always sits. Now let's see if this will fit your thimble-finger," and Mrs. Freeman held out a little shining steel thimble, and fitted it on Anne's finger. "It's just right," she said. "That is a little present for you, Anne; to go with the work-case that Mrs. Pierce gave you."

"Thank you," said Anne in a very low voice, looking at the pretty thimble, and wondering if Rose had told her mother about her trying to take the wooden doll from Millicent. "I'll always keep it," she said, looking up into the friendly face.

"Here is your work, my dear. Now set your stitches right along the basting, and set them evenly and as small as possible," and Mrs. Freeman handed Anne the strips of dimity. "But about your thimble, Anne," she continued. "I shall be better pleased if some time, when you perhaps have a thimble of silver, or have outgrown this one, you will give it to some other child who is learning to sew and has no thimble. We mustn't plan to keep gifts always, even if we do prize them. Sometimes it is best to pass them on."

Anne was quite sure that Mrs. Freeman meant that she ought to give the wooden doll to Millicent.

"I gave my coral beads, that Mistress Starkweather gave me, to the Indian girl," she said, wishing in some way to prove that she was not selfish.

"That was quite right, and I am sure that Mrs. Starkweather will tell you so," responded Mrs. Freeman.

Anne stitched away, setting her stitches very carefully. But she felt unhappy. She had quite forgotten the pleasant game with Frederick, the book that she was to write for Aunt Martha, and even the delightful fact that she was sewing on the pretty dimity dress, and had a new thimble of shining steel. All that she could think of was that she was sure that Mrs. Freeman and Rose believed her to be a selfish and ungrateful girl. "They think I want to keep everything," she said to herself. The July day grew very warm. Mrs. Freeman leaned back in her comfortable chair, closed her eyes, and indulged in a little nap. Anne's dark head began to nod, the pretty dimity slipped from her fingers to the floor, and the new thimble fell off and rolled under the table. Anne had gone fast asleep.

Rose, looking in at the chamber door, smiled to herself, tiptoed gently in and picked up the dimity dress and carried it to her own room, where Millicent was having her afternoon nap on her sister's bed. "I'll stitch up these seams while Anne's asleep," thought the kind-hearted girl, "and I'll tell her that we have a family of fairies living in this house who do things for people. I wonder if Anne ever heard of fairies?"

Mrs. Freeman was the first to wake, and, noticing that Anne's work had vanished, smiled to herself, quite sure that Rose had taken it. It was some time later when Rose brought it back and laid the thin goods on Anne's lap.

"Oh," exclaimed Anne, waking suddenly. "I dreamed of 'Martha Stoddard,'" and then, noticing the smile fade from Rose's face, Anne wished that she had not spoken, for she felt that Rose would be sure that she was still blaming little Millicent, who entered the room that very moment holding the wooden doll.

"Where did you get the wooden doll, dear?" Mrs. Freeman asked.

"Anne gave it to me," replied Millicent.

"O-oh!" Anne exclaimed impulsively, only to be sorry the next moment that she had not kept silent, for Mrs. Freeman looked up questioningly.

"Didn't you give the doll to Millicent, Anne?" she asked.

Millicent looked as if she wondered why Anne had said "Oh!" and Rose looked at her wonderingly. She could not understand why Anne should not want Millicent to have the doll, and Rose began to think that Anne was indeed selfish and ungrateful, and Anne knew what her friend was thinking, and tried hard not to cry.

"You let me have it, Anne, didn't you?" Millicent said confidently, and Anne, feeling as if she was parting from her dearest friend, managed to say: "Yes."

Mrs. Freeman's face brightened. "What is the doll's name?" she asked.

"I called her 'Martha Stoddard,'" Anne replied.

"I've named her over," said Millicent. "I've named her 'Anne Rose,' and I like her best of all my dolls."

"Have you thanked Anne for giving you her doll?" asked Mrs. Freeman.

"I'm going to give her one of mine back," declared Millicent. "I'm going to give her Miss Fillosee Follosee."

Anne wanted to cry out that she didn't want any other doll, that she wanted her own dear "Martha Stoddard," but she kept silent.

CHAPTER XV

AMOS APPEARS

ANNE picked up her thimble and said: "I'm sorry I went to sleep. I sewed only a little."

"Let me see," and Mrs. Freeman picked up the dress, and looked at the neatly stitched seams. "These seams are all stitched," she said smilingly.

Anne looked at them in surprise. "Did you do them?" she asked.

Mrs. Freeman shook her head. "No," she replied; "you see, I went to sleep, and awoke only a few moments since."

Anne hardly knew what to make of this, for she was quite sure that she had waked when Rose entered the room.

"P'raps it's fairies!" said little Millicent hopefully. "Don't you know about fairies, Anne?" and Millicent came close to Anne and laid the beloved "Martha" in her lap. "I'll tell you," she went on, in response to Anne's puzzled look. "Fairies are little, oh, littler than my thumb. I've never seen one, but Caroline's grandmother saw one, and real good children may see them some time."

"But how could anything so small sew?" questioned Anne.

"Fairies can do anything! "declared Millicent. "Caroline knows all about them. Let's go out in the yard where she is sitting with her sewing and get her to tell us a fairy story."

"Run along," said Mrs. Freeman. "You see you need not stay in to sew, since the seams are stitched."

Anne actually forgot "Martha Stoddard," so that when she jumped up to follow Millicent the wooden doll fell to the floor without either Anne or Millicent heeding it.

Rose smiled as she picked it up. "Fairies are useful little people sometimes," she said to her mother.

The days went very rapidly. Every morning Anne helped Rose with the household work, and sewed on the garments Mrs. Freeman basted for her. Every day, too, she wrote in the book for Aunt Martha. Rose made tiny sketches on many pages: of a wasp's nest, of Anne riding "Range," of Aunt Anne Rose; and here and there were little landscapes. Anne had made up her mind to let Millicent keep the wooden doll, but she sometimes wished that she had left "Martha Stoddard" safe at home in Province Town.

Beside the work there were games of bowls on the green back of the house, and pleasant walks about the town. Rose and Anne had made several visits to Mistress Mason, and Anne had already purchased a fine pewter pitcher to take home to Aunt Martha, and was knitting a warm scarf for Uncle Enos. She had not spent all of her money, and planned to buy a wonderful blue silk sash, which Mistress Mason had shown the girls on one of their visits, as a gift for Amanda. She had sent a letter to Aunt Martha Stoddard by a Province Town fisherman known to the Freemans, and the time was near when "The Yankee Hero," of which Anne's father was first mate, was due in Boston.

"Like as not your father's vessel will bring a fine prize into harbor," Frederick said one morning as he and Anne were teaching Millicent to bowl, "unless some English frigate has captured her," he added.

All up and down the coast English vessels were on the alert to seize American ships; but the American vessels were also on the outlook and had captured many of the enemy's ships.

"They'll not capture 'The Yankee Hero,' " declared Anne. "She's sailed by Province Town sailors," and Anne gave her head a little toss, as if to say that Province Town sailors were the best in the world, as she indeed thought they were.

Frederick laughed pleasantly. "You think a good deal of that old sand heap," he replied.

Anne held a ball ready to roll, but at Frederick's remark she dropped it, and stood looking at him angrily.

"It's your turn!" he reminded her, looking at her in surprise.

"It's not an old sand heap. It's the loveliest place in the world. You can see twice as much salt water there as you can in Boston," she declared.

"So you can," agreed Frederick, "but it's a sand heap just the same. A good place to catch cod, though."

"Want to see my work shop?" the boy asked when they were all tired of bowling. "Father's given me some fine pieces of wood, and I'm making a sled for Millicent to play with next winter."

Frederick's workshop was a corner of the carriage-house, where the fine chaise stood, and he had a work-bench there well supplied with tools, and spent many happy hours over his work.

"I'm going to have a shipyard and build ships," he told Anne. "See this little model!" and he held up a tiny wooden ship, fully rigged, with a little American flag fastened at the top of the mainmast. "Rose made that flag," he said proudly. "See, there's a star for each colony, thirteen of 'em."

Almost every day Anne and Rose walked to the wharves with Mr. Freeman to hear if there was any news of "The Yankee Hero." It was the very last day of July when Mr. Freeman said, as they walked down the wharf, "There's a Province Town schooner in har-bor, Anne— 'The Sea Gull.' She came for a new main-sail and will probably sail when the tide serves. There's a boat from her now, headed for my wharf."

Anne did not know that Amos Cary was on board the "Sea Gull," but she was eager to see any one who came from the place Frederick had called "the old sand heap," and watched the boat from the schooner as it came swiftly toward the Freeman wharf.

"Oh!" she exclaimed suddenly, and ran further out on the pier, quickly followed by Rose. "It looks just like Amos Cary's head. Do you suppose it is?" she asked turning to Rose.

"If it is, Amos is probably with it," Rose answered laughingly. "I suppose Amos is Amanda's brother, who came to Brewster with you. Is it that red-headed boy sitting in the bow?"

"Yes, yes!" answered Anne, fairly jumping up and down in her excitement.

Amos was now near enough to recognize Anne, and took off his cap and waved it gaily. The boat drew up to the wharf, but Amos did not jump out as Anne expected.

"I can't," he explained. "Father told Captain Nash not to let me set foot on shore," and Amos grinned as if he was delighted at what his father thought would be discipline. "I'm going to be on the 'Sea Gull' for months; maybe a whole year! Isn't that fine?"

"Jump out, Amos," said Captain Nash.

"But father said I wasn't to step foot on shore," responded the surprised boy.

"Unless I told you to," added the captain, and Amos scrambled up onto the wharf a little disappointed at the permission. "Mr. Freeman has invited you to dinner," added the captain, "but you must be here at the wharf at two sharp."

"Yes, indeed, sir," Amos answered promptly, looking back almost reluctantly toward the boat.

"Born for a sailor," the captain said to Mr. Freeman, as Amos walked with Anne and Rose toward the Freemans' house. He answered Anne's questions about Aunt Martha, Uncle Enos, Amanda and the Starkweathers, and listened to her account of the wonderful journey to Boston.

"Wasn't it great to be shut up in that dark room!" he exclaimed, when Anne told him of Bill Mains' mistake. "Wish I'd been there. But maybe the 'Sea Gull' will run afoul of a pirate ship before long," he concluded hopefully.

When Anne introduced him to Mrs. Freeman Amos took off his cap and bowed very politely, as he had noticed Captain Nash do. Frederick and he became friends instantly, and Amos was taken out to the workshop to see the model ship which had the American flag fastened to its mainmast, and he listened to Frederick's plans for building ships approvingly.

"Maybe I'll sail one of your vessels for you," he said. "I'm going to learn navigation. I'm not planning to be on shore much after this, I can tell you."

Frederick listened enviously; he thought Amos was a very fortunate boy to be going for a year's voyage on the "Sea Gull."

CHAPTER XVI

AN UNEXPECTED VISITOR

"I'll bring you some coral beads, Anne," Amos promised as he said good-bye, and started back for the wharf. Frederick went with him, and listened admiringly to Amos's plans of all he meant to see and do. Frederick began to think that it would be better to go to sea than to build ships. He watched the "Sea Gull's" sails as they caught the wind, and his eyes followed the little vessel until it looked not unlike the white-winged bird whose name it bore.

As he entered the yard Rose came down the path to meet him. She had a small package in her hand.

"I want you to do something for me, Fred," she said, "and I don't want any one, especially Anne and Millicent, to know anything about it."

This sounded interesting to Frederick, and he looked up hopefully. Perhaps there was some message to be carried from Boston to the American troops in New York, and that he, Frederick Freeman, had been selected to carry it. Probably it was wrapped up in that package which Rose held so carefully. Why, it would be a greater adventure than any Amos Cary would encounter on the "Sea Gull."

"Is it in that package, Rose?" he asked eagerly.

"How did you guess?" and Rose looked at her small brother in surprise.

"Come on out to the carriage-house, and tell me when you want me to start," and Frederick grasped Rose's arm and hurried her along. "When do you want me to start?" he asked.

"Why, right away," answered Rose in rather a puzzled tone.

The brother and sister entered the carriage-house, and Frederick led the way to the corner where his work-bench stood, and they sat down.

"Nobody will hear us here," said Frederick in a mysterious whisper, looking sharply about the room.

"Oh, Fred! I do believe that you are making believe that you are a Tory spy in danger of capture," laughed Rose.

"Indeed I'm not! I wouldn't make believe be a spy," responded the boy scornfully. "I'm a loyal messenger, ready to carry news to General Washington!"

"Here is the message," and Rose handed her brother the package.

Frederick took it with shining eyes, and held it closely.

"Oh, Rose, is it truly? And where am I to take it?" he asked.

"Why, Fred, you 'pretend' splendidly," said his sister. "I suppose you'd really like to be messenger for Washington, but that isn't it, you know. Just unroll that package and tell me how good a doll you can make."

"Make a doll!" Fred flung the little bundle to the floor and looked ready to cry. "I suppose you think it's funny to make me believe I could do something to help Washington, when you really just had an old wooden doll to show me."

"Now, Fred," and Rose put her hand on her brother's shoulder, "own up that I didn't say a word to make you imagine such a thing. You know I didn't! I asked you if you would do something for me, and not let any one know."

"Well, I might have known nothing interesting would happen to me," said Frederick. "Nothing ever does," and he regarded poor "Martha Stoddard" with scornful eyes.

"I want you to make a wooden doll as nearly like this one as you can," said Rose. "Millicent has taken possession of this one, and it's the only doll Anne has, and I'm sure that she doesn't want Millicent to have it. I thought if you could make one just like it that Millicent would like the new one better, and then Anne could have her own."

"All right," but Fred's voice was a little surly.

"And as for nothing happening to you, Fred, you ought to be thankful that nothing does happen, and that we are all safe and well. Suppose the British had won the battles at Concord and Lexington and

Bunker Hill," and Rose looked at her small brother more sternly than ever before. "I could tell you of something very pleasant that is going to happen to you," she concluded.

"What is it, Rose?" and Fred was again eager and hopeful.

But Rose shook her head. "You just wait and see. Make the wooden doll. I'll tell you when the doll is finished," and she picked "Martha" up from the floor where Frederick had dropped her.

"Can't I keep her for a pattern?" asked Frederick.

"Yes. Anne and Millicent are making paper dolls, and they won't miss her for a little while, but bring her in before supper time."

"All right," and Frederick nodded cheerfully. He was already looking over his stock of wood for suitable pieces for the new doll, and wondering what the pleasant surprise would be.

Millicent could cut out very queer little dolls, and she and Anne were quite happy together under the big horse-chestnut tree until Anne said: "Where is my wooden doll, Millicent?"

"It's mine; my Anne Rose," said little Millicent placidly. "I don't know where she is. I guess she's lost," and Millicent carefully folded a piece of paper to cut another doll.

"Lost!" Anne repeated.

"Yes," agreed Millicent, indifferently. "I guess she is; p'raps she isn't, though."

Anne remembered Caroline's story of elves, and was quite sure that her head was filled with them, for she felt as if she wanted to shake Millicent, and at the thought that her dear "Martha" was really lost Anne began to cry.

Millicent put down the scissors and paper, and looked at Anne with startled eyes, and then she began to cry. Rose came running out from the carriage-house.

"What is the matter, dear?" and she kneeled down beside her little sister. But Millicent sobbed on.

"Tell me, Anne," and she turned toward her little visitor.

"Millicent has lost 'Martha Stoddard,' " Anne managed to reply, wiping her eyes, and feeling very much ashamed that Rose should have seen her cry.

"Nonsense! The doll isn't lost. I saw it a minute ago. Come, Millicent; I'll go with you and Anne for a little walk toward King's Chapel," and Rose held out a hand to each of the girls.

"Rose," exclaimed Anne suddenly, "I know that you think I'm selfish about 'Martha Stoddard,' but Rose, listen!" and Anne looked up pleadingly into her friend's face. "When I was a little girl, not as large as Millicent, and my mother had died, and my father and I were all alone, he made me that wooden doll! I never had anything else to play with until I went to live with Aunt Martha. It isn't just a doll, Rose; it's—why, it's most like a real person," and Anne's voice sounded as if it was hard work to keep back the tears.

"You ought to have told me before," replied Rose kindly. "You see, Millicent is too little to understand, and we all love her and don't like to make her unhappy. 'Martha' is all right, and you shall have her safely back, dear," and Rose's voice was even more kind and friendly than usual as she told Anne of the new doll that Fred was making for Millicent.

"A new doll!" exclaimed Millicent happily, and could hardly wait for the time when Fred would finish it.

"So there goes my great secret!" laughed Rose. Anne was looking quite her happy self again, and Millicent was skipping along quite forgetting that she had ever wanted the wooden doll from Province Town.

"I don't believe I like secrets anyway," continued Rose; "let's go back to the carriage-house and watch Fred make the new doll, and I'll bring out the clothes I have made to dress it."

Frederick looked up from his work in surprise when the girls entered the carriage-house. "Thought it was a secret!" he exclaimed.

"No more secrets in this family," declared Rose.

"Glad to hear it. Now I can know what's going to happen to me," responded Fred.

"Of course you can. Father has to go to Salem next week and he is going to take you with him."

"Nothing will happen in driving to Salem in the morning and back at night," said Frederick, a little scornfully.

"Wait and see!" and Rose nodded so hopefully that Frederick wondered to himself if she had really told him all she knew about his father's plans.

While the children were in the carriage-house they heard the clatter of horses' hoofs on the driveway.

"Look!" exclaimed Frederick. "There's a man and a woman riding into our yard. Why, the woman is riding that black colt that brought you home."

But Rose and Anne had not waited for the end of Frederick's exclamation. Looking out they had seen the pretty black colt, and on its back a slight figure in a brown dress sitting very straight indeed, and wearing a hat of plaited straw with a brown ribbon—a hat exactly like the one Anne was so proud of.

There was a chorus of "Aunt Anne Rose! Aunt Anne Rose!" in which Millicent and Frederick joined, as the children ran out to welcome the unexpected visitors.

"I am here, too!" said Mr. Pierce laughingly.

The visitors were warmly welcomed by Mr. and Mrs. Freeman.

"I couldn't be satisfied, after this fine saddle came, until I had taken a journey," declared Aunt Anne Rose, with a happy little laugh. "And my boys were sure that they could keep house without us, so Silas and I started off. Having nieces to visit I felt as if I must come."

"Anne Rose has never been in Boston before, and she thinks it must be as large as London itself," said Mr. Pierce.

"There are indeed many places to see," said Mrs. Freeman, "and it will be a great pleasure for us to show them to Mrs. Pierce."

"There is Mistress Mason's shop," suggested Anne.

"And Governor Hancock's fine house," added Rose.

"And the wharves and shipyards," said Frederick.

As they talked the little party moved toward the house. Rose ran to the kitchen to help Caroline prepare an early supper, and Mrs. Freeman sent Anne to show the visitors to the big spare chamber.

"I wear my fine hat every day," said Anne, as she and Aunt Anne Rose went up the stairs together.

"I really think that we must take Anne back to Scituate with us," said Mr. Pierce. "What do you say, Anne?"

"My father's ship may come any day now," answered the little girl, "and then we must go home to Province Town."

It seemed to Anne as if Mrs. Pierce's face grew very grave, and she wondered to herself if Aunt Anne Rose would really like to have her live with them.

"Your cheeks are just as red, and your eyes shine; you look just like a girl, Aunt Anne Rose," she said admiringly, as Mrs. Pierce took off her hat and brushed her pretty black hair, that waved back from her face.

"It's because I'm on a visit," declared Mrs. Pierce, "and a visit to Boston. I've always wanted to come, and here I am! Everybody looks young and pretty when she is happy, Anne. But I'm not young. I'm past forty, and I never was pretty," and the dark-eyed little woman smiled radiantly, as if everything in life was planned just right.

The Pierces declared that they could stay only two days, so that evening many plans were made that they should fill the time with as much pleasure as possible. Mr. Pierce had some business to attend to with various merchants, and Anne and Rose were eager to show Mrs. Pierce the shops, the fine houses and churches; and directly after breakfast the next morning Mrs. Freeman sent them all off. Millicent was quite happy to stay with Frederick and watch him finish the wooden doll, while Rose and Anne, with Aunt Anne Rose between them, started off to visit Mistress Mason's shop, where Mrs. Pierce insisted on buying the largest of the fine dolls as a present for little Millicent, a pink silk sash for Anne and a lace collar for Rose.

"I want you girls to think often of your new aunt," she said. "And I am hoping that when Anne's father comes he will decide to bring her to visit us. I have written a letter to him, Anne, and I will give it to you. You must hand it to him, and tell him that you would like to come."

"Yes, ma'am," answered the little girl, but not very eagerly. For Anne was now counting the hours until the "Yankee Hero" should reach Boston harbor, and when she and her dear father could sail off to Province Town and tell Aunt Martha all about the wonderful visit, and give Amanda the blue silk sash. She almost wished that Aunt Anne Rose had not told her about the letter.

CHAPTER XVII

THE STRANGE SCHOONER

On the morning when Mr. and Mrs. Pierce started for home, Rose and Anne went to Mistress Mason's shop on an errand. As they walked along the street Rose exclaimed suddenly: "Anne, look! There is one of father's best friends!" And Anne looked up to see a gentleman, wearing a cocked hat and red cloak, coming toward them. He was very erect and his wig was tied with a narrow ribbon.

"Good-morning, Mistress Rose," he said, and Anne thought to herself that his voice was very kind and pleasant.

"Good-morning, Mr. Adams," Rose responded. "This is Anne Nelson from Province Town."

The friendly smile now rested on Anne. "Let me see; was there not a little maid from Province Town who helped the cause of Liberty by carrying a message to Newburyport?" he asked, clasping her hand.

Anne looked up at him and smiled. "I went with Uncle Enos," she answered.

"So you did! And now you are a visitor in Boston, as I am myself, for my family are now living in Dedham," he responded pleasantly, and, with a friendly message

171

for Mr. Freeman, he bade the girls good-bye, and walked on.

"That is Mr. Samuel Adams," explained Rose; "he came from Philadelphia but a few days ago. He signed the Declaration of Independence, Anne. And father says had it not been for Samuel Adams 'twould have been years before Congress would have come to so great a decision."

"And to think he knew of me!" said Anne.

"He knows of everybody who helped even a little bit toward American independence," said Rose. "Mr. Adams goes back to Philadelphia in September. 'Twill be a fine thing to write in your book, Anne, that you have spoken to him," said Rose, "and very likely your father will be pleased to have you go and stay with Mrs. Pierce. It's so much nearer Boston than Province Town, and the Pierces have such a pleasant house."

"It's not so pleasant as my Aunt Martha's," declared Anne loyally.

It seemed to Rose that it would be a very fortunate thing for her little friend to live with Aunt Anne Rose, and she could not understand Anne's eagerness to return to Province Town.

"May we not walk down to the wharf, Rose?" Anne asked eagerly. "Your father may have news of the ship."

But Mr. Freeman only shook his head, a little soberly, Anne thought, and the day passed without any sight or news of the "Yankee Hero."

Anne was not very happy that day. She wondered what would happen to her father if the English had captured his ship, and wished with all her heart that she was with Aunt Martha Stoddard. That night she dreamed of a fairy hid beneath her pillow, and that it whispered to her, "There is your father! Right beside the bed," and when she awoke the next morning Anne said to herself, "I feel happy, but I don't know why," and then decided that a good fairy had visited her. But when she went down-stairs, there in the front hall stood a dark man smiling as Anne exclaimed, "My father!"

For the "Yankee Hero" had arrived in the early evening of the previous night, and John Nelson had lost no time in making his way to Mr. Freeman's house, hoping for news of Anne. And he had tiptoed into her room for a look at his little daughter, just as the fairy whispered.

There was so much for Anne to tell him! John Nelson looked very grave when he heard of Anne's running away in the night.

"But Uncle Enos and Aunt Martha know that I believed they no longer wanted me," pleaded Anne. "And, oh, father, Aunt Martha said I was not to go to Brewster and journey to Boston with the Freemans to see you."

Anne had not known that her father could be so stern.

"You might never have been heard from, Anne, starting off like that. I do not know if Mistress Stoddard will be willing to again take charge of you," he said.

But after Rose had told him the story of their journey, of Anne's courage when they believed themselves prisoners in the house in the woods, and had said that it was really Amanda Cary's fault more than Anne's that she had run away, Mr. Nelson was quite ready to forgive her.

"I am glad indeed that my little girl has a good friend in Mrs. Pierce," said Mr. Nelson, after he had read Aunt Anne Rose's letter, "but I think we must go to Province Town at the first opportunity."

Anne now felt that there was nothing to wish for. With her dear father safe on shore, and the prospect of soon sailing away to Province Town she was quite happy.

"You must make Rose a fine present, Anne," he said one day as they came down King Street.

"I heard her say once that she hoped some day to have a gold ring," replied Anne.

"You shall give her one," said Mr. Nelson.

"I'll give it to her when I say good-bye," said Anne as they walked toward home.

"That may be to-morrow," responded Mr. Nelson, "for Mr. Freeman says that not a boat from Truro, Wellfleet or Province Town has come in to Boston for a week, so if the wind favors, 'tis like to-morrow will give us a chance for a passage."

Rose was on the porch, and as she watched Anne come up the path thought to herself that she would be very lonely without the little maid from Province Town.

"Captain Starkweather from Province Town is at father's wharf" she said, "and I had half a mind to tell him not to take any passengers back to Province Town, for father says he will start back when the tide serves very early to-morrow morning."

Mr. Nelson hurried away to the wharves, and Anne and Rose went up to the attic for Anne's book. "For I suppose we must pack up your things to-night," Rose said. "Your father has bought you a fine portmanteau. It's in your room now."

Anne picked up the book, and was eager to hurry to her room to see the new bag, but Rose detained her a moment.

"Why, Anne," she exclaimed, "you have left out the most important thing."

"What did I leave out?" questioned Anne.

"Why, about Amanda!" replied Rose. "You started this on purpose for Mistress Stoddard, so that she could know all about your running away."

"Oh," said Anne, in a tone of relief, "then I haven't forgotten anything. You see, Rose, Amanda told Aunt Martha all about it, so it's all right."

Rose looked at her little friend for a moment as if she were going to scold her, then she began to smile, and leaning down kissed the little girl's cheek.

"You know how to be a friend, Anne," she said, "and I'm sure Amanda will never do another hateful thing to you."

"Captain Starkweather says he'll take me to Province Town to see his boys some time," Frederick announced as the family gathered at the supper table, "and Anne's father tells me that if I go to Salem to-morrow I'll see ships that go to all parts of the world."

"That is true, my son," replied his father. "There's a ship now in Salem just arrived from Cadiz with a load of salt, and another with tea and silks from China. 'Twas great good fortune that they reached harbor safely. They would have been a fine prize for some British ship."

The Freemans all went down to the wharf with Anne the next morning. The fine portmanteau, filled with Anne's new clothing and with her gifts for the Province Town friends, was placed carefully in the little cabin. Captain Starkweather had already hoisted the sloop's mainsail, and gave Anne a warm welcome as her father helped her on board.

"Good-bye, good-bye, dear Rose," Anne called back.

As the sloop swung off from the wharf and the little girl looked back toward the friends who had been so kind to her there was a little mist in her eyes.

"It's good luck indeed to have this favoring wind," said Captain Starkweather, as the boat moved swiftly down the harbor. "I doubt not Amanda Cary is on the beach already hoping we may have sailed at midnight," and the Captain nodded smilingly toward Anne. "What are you watching so sharply, John?" he asked, for Mr. Nelson, shading his eyes with one hand, was watching a small schooner.

"Why, I'm wondering a bit about that schooner," he replied. "Her sails were hoisted and her anchor up when we left the wharf, and she's kept the same course. She couldn't be after us right in Boston harbor, but I don't like her keeping so close."

"'Tis hard work to know friends from foes on land or sea these days," said Captain Starkweather a little anxiously. For several fishermen had recently been captured by English vessels, the men taken to England, and their boats kept by the captors.

"Hoist the jib, John," directed the captain. "We'll sail away from that craft; I don't like her company."

Up went the jib, but the sloop did not increase the distance from the schooner. Both boats had now left Boston harbor well behind them. The sloop could not hope for any help now if the schooner really meant to capture it.

"There are guns on that schooner," exclaimed John Nelson. "Go into the cabin, Anne, and don't come out until I tell you to. Remember, stay in the cabin," and almost before she realized what had happened Anne found herself in the sloop's cabin, and the little door shut. A moment later she heard the bang! bang! of a gun, and felt the boat swing heavily to one side.

CHAPTER XVIII

A GREAT ADVENTURE

ANNE's first impulse was to open the cabin door, but she had learned one lesson by her runaway journey—to obey and wait. It was very hard for the little girl to keep quiet, for she could hear her father's voice, and that of Captain Starkweather, and loud commands in strange voices, and the sloop seemed to be moving this way and that as if it had lost its pilot.

"We are captured by that English boat; I know we are," Anne whispered to herself.

And that was really what had happened. The English schooner had sent a shot through Captain Starkweather's fine new mainsail, followed by a command to lay to, and before Mr. Nelson had had time to fasten the door of the cabin, the schooner was abreast of the sloop and in a few moments the Province Town boat was taken in tow by the English schooner, and Mr. Nelson and Captain Starkweather found themselves prisoners.

"Leave 'em on deck, but make sure they can't move hands or feet," Anne heard a rough voice command, and there was the sound of scuffling feet, and gradually the noise ceased; and all that Anne could hear was a faint murmur of voices, and the ripple of the water against the side of the boat. These sounds gradually ceased, and the frightened child realized that the wind had died away, and that the boats were becalmed. She peered out of the little cabin window and saw that the English boat was very near. The tide sent the sloop close to the schooner, and now Anne could hear voices very plainly.

"Pull in that tow line, and make fast to the sloop," she heard the same gruff voice command, and in a few moments the sloop lay beside the schooner.

"I could get on board just as easy," Anne thought, and wondered if her father would tell the English that his little daughter was in the sloop's cabin.

Poor John Nelson, lying on the schooner's deck, tied hand and foot, feared every moment that his conquerors would discover that there was another passenger on board the boat. "They would not harm my little maid," he assured himself, "but there is food and water in the sloop's cabin, and Anne is best off there."

Both he and Captain Starkweather hoped that some American vessel might come to their rescue. But now that the wind had died away there was no chance of that for the present.

"A midsummer calm. May be stuck here for twenty-four hours," Anne heard a grumbling voice declare.

The long summer day dragged by. Anne opened the lunch basket, but had little appetite. At sunset there was a ripple of wind and the two boats, side by side, moved a short distance.

Anne, shut up in the tiny cabin, had come to a great resolve. "Father told me to stay here, but if I could creep aboard the schooner and untie the cords, then father and Captain Starkweather could get free," she thought. And the more she thought of it, the more sure she was that she could do it.

The twilight deepened, and now Anne ventured to push open the cabin door a little way. The sailors were in the forecastle, but Anne could see a dark figure in the stern of the schooner. She ventured out and softly closed the cabin door. Now, on her hands and knees, the little girl crept across the little space toward the side of the schooner. It looked like a black wall, but not very high above her, and there were ropes; and Anne was used to boats. Grasping a rope she drew herself up, hand over hand, until she could reach the deck-rail. Now she gave a swift glance toward the dark figure at the stern. "I do believe he's asleep," she thought, and Anne now pulled herself to the top of the rail and dropped noiselessly to the deck of the schooner. For a few moments she cowered in the shadow, and then looked anxiously about. Near the cabin she could see two black shadows, and knew that they were her father and Captain Starkweather.

Keeping close in the shadow Anne crept along the deck. But, noiseless as her progress had been, Anne had been seen the moment her little figure reached the top of the deck rail. John Nelson's keen eyes, staring into the summer night, had recognized his little daughter, and instantly realized that Anne meant to help them. He held his breath for fear that some sharp ear had caught a sound, and then whispered to his companion, "Don't move, or call out, captain; Anne is on deck and will help us."

The little girl was now close beside her father. "Feet first, Anne," he whispered, and Anne's eager fingers pulled and worked at the tough knots so securely tied until they loosened, and John Nelson could move his feet. Her father did not dare even whisper again. He longed to tell her to hurry, but dared not speak. Anne was now tugging and twisting at the rope which held her father's wrists, and managed to loosen it so that he could work his hands free. Then they both began to loosen Captain Starkweather's cords, and in a few minutes he too was free. The same thought was running through the minds of both men: If a girl like Anne had such courage, why couldn't two sailors make a prize of this good English boat?

"Go back to the sloop's cabin, Anne. We'll follow," whispered her father. And Anne obeyed. She was not afraid now. How easy it had been, she thought happily, as she slid down the rope to the sloop's deck, and found herself again in the little cabin.

The dark figure, dozing at the schooner's helm, did not see the two creeping men who so suddenly were upon him. A twisted scarf over his mouth, and no sound to warn his mates, his hands and feet bound with the very cords that had secured his prisoners, he was left a captive. Then John Nelson and Captain Starkweather sped toward the forecastle; the open hatchway was closed so quickly that the men below hardly realized what had happened, and it was securely fastened before they could help themselves.

"The breeze is coming," declared Captain Starkweather. "Shall we put back to Boston, John? We'll not know what to do with this craft in Province Town."

"A good night's work this, and Boston folk will be glad to see this English 'Sea Bird' come in to her harbor. 'Tis the same craft that has caused so much trouble to fishing boats. I'll bring Anne on board," and John Nelson ran to the schooner's side and called, "Anne! Anne!" A moment later and he lifted his little daughter to the deck of the schooner.

"You are a brave child," declared Captain Starkweather. "This schooner is really your prize, for 'tis by your courage that we have taken her."

The schooner's course was changed, and, the wind increasing, she swept off toward Boston harbor.

"'Twill be a good tale for Mr. Samuel Adams to hear," said Captain Starkweather, "and you will indeed be proud of your little daughter, John. I doubt not but this will be printed in the Boston papers, and news of it sent to General Washington himself."

"YOU ARE THE BRAVEST GIRL IN THE COLONY"

It was hardly sunrise when the "Sea Bird," towing Captain Starkweather's sloop, came to anchor off the Freemans' wharf. John Nelson's hail to a friendly fisherman brought a number of boats alongside, and when he had told them of how the capture was made a chorus of huzzas filled the air. The news was carried to the other vessels in the harbor, and the "Sea Bird" was soon surrounded by small boats. One of these boats pulled for the shore, and its crew spread the news that a little girl and two sailors from Province Town had captured and brought into harbor a fine English schooner. Mr. Freeman heard the news on his way to the wharf, and saw the crew of the "Sea Bird" being marched up the street under a strong guard. The church bells were rung, and when John Nelson and Anne reached shore they were welcomed by cheers.

Rose came hurrying through the crowd.

"Oh, Anne!" she exclaimed. "Here is Mr. Samuel Adams waiting to speak to you! You are the bravest girl in the colony."

" 'Twill be a wonderful thing to tell Amanda," said Anne happily. "Even Amos could hope for no finer adventure."

"There'll be prize money," added Frederick. I heard my father say that there'll be a large sum for you and your father and for Captain Starkweather."

It was a week later when they sailed once more for Province Town. It was decided that it would be safer to leave the harbor at nightfall, when there would be a better chance of the sloop not being recognized and followed by some watchful craft lurking in the lower harbor. This time the little cabin was nearly filled, for Captain Starkweather was taking gifts to each one of his six boys, beside wonderful packages for their mother, and Anne and her father could hardly wait for the time when Uncle Enos and Aunt Martha should see the set of lustre ware, the fine pewter, and the boxes of figs, dates, jellies and sweets which they were taking to Province Town.

CHAPTER XIX

"HOMEWARD BOUND"

Captain Starkweather had renamed his sloop.
The old name had been painted out, and now, on each
side of the boat, in gilt letters on a white scroll the new
name "Anne Nelson" could be seen.

The little craft was anchored off the Freeman wharf,
and at early twilight Mr. Nelson and Anne said their
good-byes to the Freemans, and put off in the sloop's
tender. Captain Starkweather was on board the sloop,
and as noiselessly as possible they made ready to start.

The favoring winds swept the little craft along, and
as the sun came smiling up from the far horizon Anne
awoke, and was quite ready for the crackers, boiled eggs
and doughnuts that Mrs. Freeman had packed for
their breakfast.

The long "arm" of land now stretched out as if to welcome the returning voyagers, and the sloop ran in
beside the little pier just as Captain Enos and Jimmie
Starkweather came down the beach.

"Been watching your craft since sunup," declared
Uncle Enos. "What's kept you in Boston so long, Starkweather? We began to worry about you, John, and
feared some ill news of our little maid."

Anne did not wait to hear her father tell the story of their great adventure, but ran swiftly up the path toward home. Aunt Martha was standing in the doorway, and as Anne saw the loving smile and felt the kind arms encircle her she was indeed sure that this was home, and that the most fortunate thing that had ever befallen her had been the welcome Aunt Martha had given her two years before, when she had come to that very door asking for shelter.

How much there was to tell! And how Aunt Martha exclaimed over the adventures of her little maid, and thanked heaven that she was safely back in Province Town.

Then when Uncle Enos and John Nelson came up the path, each wheeling a barrow filled with the fine gifts that Anne and her father had brought home, then indeed did Mistress Stoddard declare that it was enough to make one believe in good fairies. And that reminded Anne of Caroline's story, which she had written down in the book.

Captain Enos put on his glasses and looked the book over admiringly.

"It should be in print," he declared; "this book is the finest thing of all, Anne. 'Twould be an excellent idea, Martha, for us to ask the neighborhood in to hear it read."

But Mrs. Stoddard shook her head, and said Anne must not think too well of what, after all, was Miss Rose Freeman's book as much as it was Anne's. "You must not overpraise our little maid," she warned Captain Enos reprovingly. But the book was ever one of Mistress Stoddard's most valued treasures, and was kept with "Pilgrim's Progress" in the big chest.

It was late in the afternoon before all the dishes, pewter, the fine new table-cloths, and the pretty brown cloth for Mistress Stoddard's new gown, were unpacked.

"This package is for Amanda," Anne said, holding up a good-sized bundle.

"For Amanda, indeed!" exclaimed Mistress Stoddard. "I'm not too sure that she deserves it. 'Twas she that sent you out into the night, thinking your Aunt Martha hard-hearted and unfair. And now a fine present for her—I do not know about it."

"Oh, Aunt Martha, Amanda didn't mean to," pleaded Anne, "and she came and told you."

Anne picked up the bundle and sped away. Down past the spring and up the sandy path toward Amanda's home she ran, hoping to meet Amanda coming to welcome her. Amanda was on the door-step with her knitting. At the sight of Anne she started up as if to run indoors, but Anne's call made her hesitate, and in a moment Anne was beside her, saying: "Amanda! Amanda! Isn't it fine that I am home again! And see, I've brought you these presents from Boston. See, Amanda!" and she held up the silk sash, and spread out the pretty dimity.

But instead of exclaiming with delight, as Anne had expected, poor Amanda dropped her work, covered her face with her hands and began to cry.

"Stop crying, Amanda Cary! You'll get spots on your lovely sash," said Anne, and Amanda's tears ceased in sudden terror lest she spoil that wonderful length of shining blue silk.

"Taste of that barley sugar, Amanda," continued Anne, opening a heart-shaped box, and helping herself to a piece. Amanda obeyed almost unconsciously, and when Mrs. Cary came to the door a little later she found the two girls sitting close together, talking and laughing.

That night after Anne was fast asleep in the little loft chamber, John Nelson told his good friends that he wished all the little settlement to share in his good fortune.

"My little maid and I have found a home and friends here," he said, "and I should like well to do some friendly thing for the people before I return to Boston."

" 'Twould be a pleasant thing for us all to have a day together, and a good dinner," suggested Mistress Stoddard, "with figs, dates, and some of those fine crackers and jellies, and of course, a good fish chowder; 'twould be a treat indeed," and so it was decided that the neighborhood should be bidden to come as the guests of John Nelson and Anne for a day's pleasuring.

"We'll spread a sail in the yard to make a shelter from the sun," suggested Captain Enos.

"I'll make the chowder myself," declared John Nelson. "Mistress Stoddard shall not be burdened with work, and I'll see that the Starkweather boys earn a shilling by helping me," and it was settled that the following Thursday should be the day.

Anne thought it the finest plan in the world, and she and Amanda brought branches of pine, and fragrant fir balsam to cover the ground under the big sail. Mrs. Stoddard insisted on spreading her two new fine table-cloths over the rough table, and on using her tall pewter pitchers.

"And Elder Haven is to have a plate and cup of china," she said proudly.

Not a boat put out from harbor on that Thursday morning, and the day was not far advanced when the guests, all wearing their Sunday best, began to come up the hill toward Captain Stoddard's house. John Nelson and Anne gave them all a warm welcome, and as they all stood together around the white covered table and Elder Haven asked a blessing to rest on them all it seemed to Anne and Amanda that it was the happiest day that Province Town had ever known.

The Stories in This Series Are:

A LITTLE MAID OF PROVINCETOWN
A LITTLE MAID OF MASSACHUSETTS COLONY
A LITTLE MAID OF NARRAGANSETT BAY
A LITTLE MAID OF OLD PHILADELPHIA
A LITTLE MAID OF OLD NEW YORK
A LITTLE MAID OF OLD CONNECTICUT
A LITTLE MAID OF TICONDEROGA
A LITTLE MAID OF VIRGINIA
A LITTLE MAID OF MARYLAND
A LITTLE MAID OF MOHAWK VALLEY
A LITTLE MAID OF OLD MAINE

Available from:
APPLEWOOD BOOKS
Bedford, MA 01730